"Thank you for turning a headache into an adventure. I developed a great enthusiasm for changing our business so that it would run more smoothly and start moving towards our Strategic Objective."
—*Lia Gianola Bland, George Gianola & Sons, Sausalito, CA*

"For years, I've been a one-man shop 'doing my thing' on my terms. Michael Gerber has awakened me to becoming customer-oriented rather than self-oriented. This has resulted in my taking steps to form a 'Franchise Prototype.' The dream is returning."
—*Ron Turner, Turner Studios, Mountain View, CA*

"My whole life has changed since enrolling in your program three months ago. Not just my business has grown (which it clearly has), but I've grown in all areas of my life."
—*Sydney Tasso, Wachters' Organic Sea Products, Santa Cruz, CA*

"We used to worry constantly. Now we've gained more confidence in our scheduling capabilities and we can estimate deadlines in a practical, realistic manner. We can spend our outside-of-business time relaxing, reading, and making final plans to enter into our primary aims. After three years of doing business here our dreams and enthusiasms are being rejuvenated."
—*Mike Hughes and Donna Duncan, Hughes Fabrication, Sunnyvale, CA*

"The impact you have had on our business is definitely a new commitment to the business, a new direction, a new focus. Sales have changed from single items to multiple sales. More business from the same amount of customers—I love it!"
—*Bert S. Bloom, The Linen Depot, San Francisco, CA*

"A note of thanks to you for developing a program that gives each person in our organization a sense of participating in the organization of the company. Working *on* our company not *in* our company is something we have been putting off for years. You made us realize just how important this is to our survival."
—*Gerald L. Headding, M. Boss, Sunnyvale, CA*

"Overall benefits include 1) a tremendously increased awareness of the problems of small businesses today, 2) a realization of the urgency of developing systems that produce results so I won't always be working, slaving in my business, 3) an expanded understanding of ways my subconscious works both for and against my objectives, and 4) an exciting philosophic commitment to your program."
—*Harriet Holmes, Mary Kay Cosmetics Sales Representative*

"Thanks to you we experience much change and positive growth in our church/business. As always we feel that there are 'answers' to our 'dilemmas' and the source for many of the answers is Michael Thomas."
—*Barry and Elaine, Wingham Ministries, Mill Valley, CA*

"Thanks for your well-timed 'push' to assist us in completing our Strategic Objective. I am enjoying our business once again. Our employees are sharing our excitement and sense of accomplishment as they assist us in the myriad of projects."
—*Laurie A. Moore, Larry's [VW] Bug Shop, Mountain View, CA*

"Now we are on the right track toward understanding what it takes to attain our Strategic Objective and Personal Aim."
—*Richard A. Jones, Medico Supply Company Inc., San Francisco, CA*

"After six months of learning, resistance, and acceptance I feel we have made a major leap into action at last, one that we can see in our business. There is so much more to do, but at least we've taken the first step."
—*Judy Creighton, Creighton's Cheese and Fine Foods, San Francisco, CA*

"We have found we accomplish more in half the time. Before we did these things the company seemed to run itself by accident. The new organization has created a much smoother atmosphere to work in and employer-employee relations are at an all-time high."
—*Steve Tingley, Steve Tingley Painting, Hayward, CA*

"As you can see by the postmark, I'm off on another junket. I'm doing exactly what I planned when I joined Michael Thomas. I'm not only getting the time off I so fervently sought, but the business is actually prospering. Morale is at an all-time high and productivity is up."
—*John W. Gross, John J. Gross, Painting and Paperhanging, San Francisco, CA*

"We have gained an immense and helpful new knowledge and approach to achieving our strategic and personal goals in life. We have a foothold on the concept that will create viability for any business concept that we involve ourselves in."
—*Joe M. Flake, Joe M. Flake & Co., Group Travel Specialists, San Rafael, CA*

"The initial strategic planning we have done has provided a clearing in which we can create the systems necessary to implement our plans. The seminars at Michael Thomas have been inspiring and useful."
—*Howard Goldman, Management Associates, Search Consultants, Santa Clara, CA*

"I'd been skipping along for seven months, in love with my commodity (marketing design) but a lamb in a lion's world. I soon realized that integrity was enough to keep me working, but not enough to build a business. Your products and seminars have provided the systems. Ultimately, however, your effectiveness lies solely with me. I'm now in a better position to join the business world—with confidence and knowledge to match the quality of my service."
—*Donna Bunce, Lasting Impressions, Palo Alto, CA*

"Your business development program continues to have a profound impact on our professional business but, more significantly, on our personal lives. After we installed and began to use systematically your cash management system, we will gross more (by more than 50%) this month than in any other month of our ten-month adventure into private practice."
—*Walter C. Saunders, Ph.D, Clinical Psychologist, San Jose, CA*

"The more I know about your program the more impressed I get. Keep telling everybody: YOUR PRODUCTS WORK.
—*Jean-Claude Potin, The Compleat Baldwin Brass Center, San Francisco, CA*

"In addition to crediting you with playing a substantial role in taking what was a subsidiary operation in the red, and turning it into a highly profitable sale, I've found the program to have had a profound impact on my life. Sitting down and truly plotting a direction for myself in all aspects of my life, and then proceeding to set a time schedule in which to achieve my goals, was an exhilarating process."
—*Don Wexler, The Pure Source, Emeryville, CA*

"Finally someone has figured out the answer to the problems that have been frustrating me for years."
—*Warren Kaufman, Natural Development Building & Remodeling, Carmel Valley, CA*

THE E-MYTH

The E-Myth

Why Most Businesses Don't Work and What To Do About It

Michael E. Gerber

■ ■

Ballinger Publishing Company, Cambridge, Massachusetts
A Subsidiary of Harper & Row, Publishers, Inc.

International Standard Book Number: 0-88730-040-5 (cl)
0-88730-362-5 (pbk)

Library of Congress Catalog Card Number: 85-4002

Printed in the United States of America

Book design by Joyce C. Weston

Library of Congress Cataloging in Publication Data

Gerber, Michael E.
  The E-myth, why most businesses don't work and what
to do about it.

  Bibliography: p.
  Includes index.
  1. Small business—Management. 2. Entrepreneur.
3. Success in business. I. O'Heffernan, Patrick. II. Title
HD62.7.G46 1985   658'.022   85-4002
ISBN 0-88730-040-5 (cl)
     0-88730-362-5 (pbk)

*To the memory of my father,
I wish he were here.*

CONTENTS

PROLOGUE

S ince *The E-Myth* first appeared in 1986, I've been privileged to receive inquiry after inquiry from entrepreneurs, would-be entrepreneurs, and people who own small businesses throughout the world—in France, Germany, England, Australia, South Korea, and Canada, as well as from every state in the United States—all of them expressing their deeply felt gratitude for what this book has meant to them. At the heart of their inquiries were the repeated questions, How can I get the help you talk about in your book? How can I put the Business Development Process to work for me in my business?

In response to that interest, we have included a request form at the back of this book that you the reader may submit to order a Complimentary Needs Analysis of your business by my company, The Michael Thomas Corporation. Using the principles outlined in this book as a model, the Needs

Analysis will help you take the first step toward a more realistic understanding of what works in your business and what doesn't; toward a more pragmatic understanding of your business as a system, rather than as a place to go to work—a system designed to give your customer what he or she wants in a way that differentiates your business from every other business around.

As you read this book, you'll discover that I hold a very specific point of view about creating a business that works. It's not a very comfortable point of view to hold. People react intensely to it, many for, many against. At the heart of this view is the indisputable fact that most businesses don't work—the people who *own* them do. Also undeniable is the fact that while most businesses run poorly in good times and bad, good businesses run well no matter what's going on outside.

The question is often asked of me, What does the successful business person know that the unsuccessful business person doesn't? The answer is, Lots. But that's not why he or she is successful. Despite common belief, people don't succeed in business because of what they know, **but because of their insatiable need to know more**. Conversely, the problem with most failing businesses is not that the owner doesn't know enough about finance, about marketing, about management, about operations—those things are easy enough to learn. The problem is that **he thinks he knows enough**. And so he spends his time trying to defend and justify what he knows, rather than to discover what he doesn't.

This book is dedicated to that process of discovery and to the business people among us who pursue it. It is intended as a guide for those who see the development of a successful business for what it really is—as an inquiry, an investigation, an active engagement with a world of forces, within us and without, that continually amaze and confound us with their awesome variety, their unending surprises, their untold complexity.

A wise person once said, "Know thyself." To that honorable dictum I can only add, Good traveling.

"To live through an impossible situation, you don't need the reflexes of a Grand Prix driver, the muscles of a Hercules, the mind of an Einstein. You simply need to know what to do."

—*Anthony Greenbank*
The Book of Survival

ACKNOWLEDGEMENTS

I would like to express my deepest gratitude to the many people with whom I've worked to produce the ideas that are presented in this book, as well as for the support needed to complete it.

To Ilene Gerber, my wife and my partner, whose passion, skill, heart, and wisdom, both in the business and out, contributed not only to the writing and thinking of this book, but to our company and its achievements, and, most importantly, to the evolution of my life, in ways too numerous to mention;

To Shana, Kim, and Hillary, my daughters, who, through their patience and love, gave me the freedom I've needed to do what I've done; and to Sam, my son, who at this writing is within one month of being born, a promise of good, good things to come;

To all my associates at MTC, through good times and bad, who, with determination, conviction, heart, and imagination have put the idea of Business Development to work in everything they've done, especially: Marsh Agobert, Paul Anderson, Andy Baldwin, Guy Bogenreif, Mary Curry Browne, Glen Burger, Kenny Cahn, Vio Chiang, Bill Creveling, Muni Cruz, Chris Doty, Janice Drescher, Tom Drew, Bud Evans, John Fandel, Marijo Franklin, Elmer Goble, Sharon Kaiser, Lisa Kobayashi, Amy Konishi, Patricia Lamski, Sid Mantel, Carolyn Martin, Jim Quinn, Mary Restor, Cammie Schmidt, Lynn Schriver, Eric Selfridge, Jay Veneaux, Bob Werner, and Sarah Wilhelm;

And to all our clients whose trust, commitment, and willingness to succeed and to fail taught us what works in the real world in a way that would have been impossible without them;

And finally, to Patrick O'Heffernan, who struggled with me through the genesis of the book to its completion with good humor and a firm hand, both of which were appreciated;

Thank you all.

INTRODUCTION

"I think that maybe inside any business, there is someone
slowly going crazy."

Joseph Heller
Something Happened

If you own a business, or if you want to own a business, this
book was written for you. It represents thousands of hours
of work we've done in thousands of small businesses over the
past ten years. It illustrates a belief created and supported by
the experiences of the countless people with whom we've
worked: *that businesses in this country simply do not
work.*

That's not because people who own and operate businesses don't work. They do. They work far more than they
should for the return they're getting. The problem is that
they're doing the *wrong* work. As a result, their businesses
end up in chaos—unmanageable, unpredictable, and unre-
warding.

Just look at the numbers.

Businesses start and fail in the United States at an
increasingly staggering rate. Every year, over 500,000

people start a business of some sort. By the end of the first year, at least 40 percent of them will be out of business. Within five years, more than 80 percent of them—400,000 —will have failed.[1]

And, if you own a business which has managed to survive for five years or more, don't breathe a sigh of relief. More than 80 percent of the enterprises that survive the first five years fail in the *second* five.

Why is this? Why do so many people go into business, only to fail? What lesson aren't they learning? Why is it that with all the information on how to be successful in business, so few people really are?

This book answers those questions. It's about four profound ideas, which, if you understand and take them to heart, will give you the power to create an extraordinarily successful business. Ignore them, and you will likely join the 200,000 people a year who pour their energy and capital into starting a business and fail, or the many others who struggle along for years simply trying to survive.

IDEA #1   There is a myth in this country—the E-Myth—which says that businesses are started by entrepreneurs risking capital to make a profit. This is simply not so. The real reasons people start businesses have little to do with entrepreneurship. But belief in the Entrepreneurial Myth is the most important factor in the devastating rate of business failure in America today. Understanding the Myth and applying that understanding can be the secret to any business's success.

IDEA #2   There's a revolution going on today in American Business, the Turn-Key Revolution. Not only is

---

1. Department of Commerce.

it changing the way we do business in this country, but it is changing who goes into business, how they do it, and the likelihood of success.

IDEA #3   At the heart of the Turn-Key Revolution is a dynamic process called business development. This process, which I call The Business Development Process when it is systematized and applied purposely by a business owner, is one of the foundations of every great company. When a company incorporates this process into its every activity and uses it to control its destiny, that company stays young and thrives. When a company ignores this process—as most do—it commits itself to "Management by Luck," stagnates and fails.

IDEA #4   The Business Development Process can be systematically applied by any business owner in a step-by-step method that incorporates the lessons of the Turn-key Revolution to the operation of his business. It then becomes a predictable way to produce success in *any* business that's willing to give it the time and attention it needs to flourish.

At The Michael Thomas Corporation, we have introduced The Business Development Process in a seven-step Business Development Program and we have seen it succeed in thousands of cases. Once applied and operating in your business, this method will give you the level of control you need to get what you want from your business.

This book, then, is about producing results. But it is *not* another "how-to-do-it" book. My experience working with people in small business has made it obvious to me that the last thing anyone needs is another business book on "how-to-do-it." Because books like that don't work.

People do. And what makes people work is *an idea worth working for*, an understanding of what needs to be done. Only when such an idea becomes firmly integrated into the way you think and operate does how-to-do-it become at all meaningful.

This book is about such an idea: *that your business is nothing more than a distinct reflection of who you are.*

If your thinking is sloppy, your business will be sloppy. If your information about what needs to be done in a business is limited, your business will reflect that limitation. If you are disorganized, your business will be disorganized. If you are greedy, your employees will be greedy, giving you less and less of themselves and constantly asking for more.

So if your business is to change—as it must to be successful—*you* must change first. For unless *you* change, your business will never be capable of giving you what you want. But once *you* change, your business will change and grow.

And the first change you need to make is in your understanding of what a business *really* is, and what it takes to make one work. Once this is grasped, your business and your life will take on a vitally new meaning. You'll begin to understand why so many people fail to get what they want from a business of their own. You'll begin to understand the almost magical opportunities available to anyone who starts a business in the right way, with a true understanding, with the necessary tools. I've seen it happen thousands of times. In every kind of business imaginable. With people who knew *nothing* about business when they started.

It not only *can* happen to you; it *will.*

Welcome. Enjoy. Prosper.

You're now on your way.

PART I

The E-Myth and American Business

1

THE ENTREPRENEURIAL MYTH

"They intoxicate themselves with work so they won't see how they really are."

Aldous Huxley

The E-Myth is the myth of the entrepreneur. It runs deep in this country and rings of the heroic. Picture the typical entrepreneur and Herculean pictures come to mind: a man or woman standing alone, wind-blown against the elements, bravely defying insurmountable odds, climbing sheer faces of treacherous rock—all to realize the dream of creating a business of one's own. The legend reeks of nobility, of lofty, extra-human efforts, of a prodigious commitment to larger-than-life ideals.

Well, while there *are* such people, my experience tells me they are rare. Of the thousands of business people I have had the opportunity to know and work with, few were *real* entrepreneurs when I met them. The vision was all but gone in most. The zest for the climb had turned into a terror of heights. The face of the rock had become something to cling to rather than to scale. Exhaustion was common, exhilaration rare.

But all of them must have once been entrepreneurs. After all, they had started their own business. There must have been some dream that drove them to take such a risk. But, if so, where was the dream now? Why had it faded? Where was the entrepreneur who had started the business?

The answer is simple: *the entrepreneur had only existed for a moment.* A fleeting second in time. And then it was gone. In most cases, forever. If the entrepreneur survived at all, it was only as a myth that grew out of a misunderstanding about who goes into business and why. A misunderstanding that has cost us dearly in this country— more than we can possibly imagine—in resources, lost opportunities, and wasted lives.

That myth, that misunderstanding, I call the E-Myth, the myth of the entrepreneur. And it finds its roots in this country in a romantic belief that businesses are started by entrepreneurs, when, in fact, most are not.

Then who does start businesses in America? And why?

The Entrepreneurial Seizure

To understand the E-Myth and the misunderstanding at its core, let's take a closer look at the person who goes into business. Not *after* he goes into business, but before.

Where were *you* before you started your business? (If you're thinking about going into business, where are you now?) If you're like 99 percent of the people I've known, *you were working for somebody else.*

What were you doing? Probably technical work, like almost everybody who goes into business. You were a carpenter, a mechanic, or a machinist. You were a bookkeeper or a poodleclipper; a draftsperson or a hairdresser; a barber or a computer programmer; a doctor or a technical writer; a graphics artist or an accountant; an interior designer or a plumber or a salesperson. But whatever your profession, *you were doing technical work.* And you were probably damn good at it. But you were doing it for somebody else.

Then one day, for no apparent reason, something happened. It might have been the weather, a birthday, or your child's graduation from high school. It might have been the paycheck you received on a Friday afternoon, or a sideways glance from the boss that just didn't sit right. It might have been a feeling that your boss didn't really appreciate your contribution to the success of his business.

It could have been anything; it doesn't matter what. But one day, for apparently no reason, *you were suddenly stricken with an Entrepreneurial Seizure.* And from that day on your life was never to be the same.

Inside your mind it sounded something like this: "What am I doing this for? Why am I working for this guy? Hell, I know as much about this business as he does. If it weren't for me, he wouldn't have a business. Any dummy can run a business. I'm working for one."

And the moment you paid attention to what you were saying and really took it to heart, your fate was sealed. The excitement of cutting the cord became your constant companion. The thought of independence followed you everywhere. The idea of being your own boss, doing your own thing, singing your own song, became delightfully irresistible.

Once you were stricken with an Entrepreneurial Seizure, there was no relief. You couldn't rid of it. You *had* to go into business.

The Fatal Assumption

In the throes of your Entrepreneurial Seizure, you fell victim to the most disastrous assumption anyone can make about going into business. It is an assumption made by *all* technicians who go into business for themselves, one that charts the course of a business—from Grand Opening to Liquidation—the moment it is made.

That Fatal Assumption is: *if you understand the technical work of a business, you understand a business that does that technical work.*

And the reason it's fatal is that it *just isn't true.* In fact, it's the root cause of most business failures!

The technical work of a business and a business that does that technical work *are two totally different things!* But the technician who starts a business fails to see this. To the technician, a business is *not* a business but *a place to go to work.*

So the carpenter becomes a contractor. The barber opens up a barber shop. The technical writer starts a technical writing business. The hairdresser starts a beauty salon. The engineer goes into the semiconductor business. The musician opens a music store. All of them believing that understanding the technical work of the business eminently qualifies them to run a business that does that kind of work.

Not true. In fact, rather than being their greatest single asset, knowing the technical work of their businesses becomes their greatest single liability. For if the technician didn't know how to *do* the technical work of the business, he would have to learn *how to get it done.* He would be forced to learn how to make the *business* work, rather than to do the work himself.

When the technician falls prey to the Fatal Assumption, the business that was supposed to *free* him from the limitations of working for somebody else actually *enslaves* him. Suddenly the job he knew how to do so well becomes one job he knows how to do *plus a dozen others he doesn't know how to do at all.*

Because although the Entrepreneurial Seizure *started* the business, it's the technician who goes to work. And suddenly the entrepreneurial dream becomes the technician's nightmare.

2

THE ENTREPRENEUR, THE MANAGER, AND THE TECHNICIAN

"Thus, in the course of his life, one man acquires many personal qualities, many personages, many 'I's' (because each, speaking for itself independently of the others says 'I,' 'me,' when it appears)."

Jean Vaysse
Toward Awakening

The Technician isn't the only problem. The problem is compounded by the fact that everybody who goes into business is actually three-people-in-one: The Entrepreneur, The Manager, *and* The Technician. Each of these personalities wants to *be* the boss. But none of them wants to *have* a boss. So they start a business together in order to *get rid of* the boss. And the conflict begins.

To show you how the problem manifests itself in all of us, let's examine the way our various internal personalities interact. Let's take a look at two personalities we're all familiar with: The Fat Guy and The Skinny Guy.

Have you ever decided to go on a diet? You're sitting in front of the television set one Saturday afternoon, watching an athletic competition, awed by the athletes' stamina and dexterity. You're eating a sandwich, your second since you sat down to watch the event two hours before. You're feeling sluggish in the face of all the action on the screen when, suddenly, somebody wakes up in you and says, "What are you doing? Look at yourself, You're Fat! You're out of shape! Do something about it!"

It has happened to us all. Somebody wakes up inside us with a totally different picture of who we should be and what we should be doing. In this case, let's call him The Skinny Guy.

Who's The Skinny Guy? He's the one who uses words like: "discipline," "exercise," "organization." The Skinny Guy is intolerant, self-righteous, a stickler for detail, a compulsive tyrant. The Skinny Guy abhors fat people. Can't stand sitting around. Needs to be on the move. Lives for action.

The Skinny Guy has just taken over. Watch out—things are about to change.

Before you know it, you're cleaning all the fattening foods out of the refrigerator. You're buying a new pair of running shoes, barbells, and sweats. Things are going to be different around here. You have a new lease on life. You plan your new physical regimen: up at five, run three miles, cold shower at six, a breakfast of wheat toast, black coffee, and half a grapefruit; then, ride your bicycle to work, home by seven, run another two miles, to bed at ten—the world's already a different place!

And you actually pull it off! By Monday night, you've lost two pounds. You go to sleep dreaming of winning the Boston Marathon. Why not? The way things are going, it's only a matter of time.

Tuesday night you get on the scale. Another pound gone! You're incredible. Gorgeous. A lean machine.

On Wednesday, you really pour it on. You work out an extra hour in the morning, an extra half-hour at night.

13

You can't wait to get on the scale. You strip down to your bare skin, shivering in the bathroom, filled with expectation of what your scale is going to tell you. You step lightly onto it, and look down. What you see is . . . *nothing.* You haven't lost an ounce. You're exactly the same as you were on Tuesday.

Dejection creeps in. You begin to feel a slight twinge of resentment. "After all that work? After all that sweat and effort? And then—nothing? It isn't fair." But you shrug it off. After all, tomorrow's another day. You go to bed, vowing to work harder on Thursday. But somehow something's changed.

You don't know what's changed until Thursday morning. It's raining. The room is cold. Something feels different. What is it? For a minute or two you can't quite put your finger on it. And then you get it: *somebody else is in your body.* It's The Fat Guy! He's back! And he doesn't want to run. As a matter of fact, he doesn't even want to get out of bed. It's cold outside. "Run? Are you kidding me?" The Fat Guy doesn't want anything to do with it. The only exercise he might be interested in is eating!

And all of a sudden you find yourself in front of the refrigerator—*inside* the refrigerator—all over the kitchen! Food is now your major interest. The Marathon is gone; the lean machine is gone; the sweats and barbells and running shoes are gone. The Fat Guy is back. He's running the show again.

It happens to all of us, time and time again. Because we've been deluded into thinking we're really *one person.* And so when The Skinny Guy decides to change things we actually believe that it's *I* who's making that decision. And when The Fat Guy wakes up and changes it all back again, we think it's *I* who's making that decision too.

But it isn't I. It's *we.*

The Skinny Guy and The Fat Guy are two totally different personalities, with different needs, different interests, and different lifestyles. That's why they don't like each other. They each want totally different things.

The problem is that when you're The Skinny Guy, you're totally consumed by *his* needs, *his* interests, *his* lifestyle. And then somethings happens—the scale disappoints you, the weather turns cold, somebody offers you a ham sandwich. At that moment, The Fat Guy, who's been waiting in the wings all this time, grabs your attention. Grabs control. *You're him again.*

In other words, when you're The Skinny Guy you're always making promises for The Fat Guy to keep. And when you're The Fat Guy, you're always making promises for The Skinny Guy to keep. Is it any wonder we have such a tough time keeping our commitments to ourselves? It's not that we're indecisive or unreliable; it's that each and every one of us is a whole set of different personalities, each with his own interests and way of doing things. Asking any one of them to defer to any of the others is inviting a battle or even a full-scale war.

Anyone who has ever experienced the conflict between The Fat Guy and The Skinny Guy knows what I mean. You can't be both; one of them *has* to lose. And they both know it.

Well, that's the kind of war going on inside the owner of every small business. But it's a three-way battle between The Entrepreneur, The Manager and The Technician. Unfortunately, it's a battle no one can win.

Understanding the differences among them will quickly explain why.

The Entrepreneur

The entrepreneurial personality turns the most trivial condition into an exceptional opportunity. The Entrepreneur is the visionary in us. The dreamer. The energy behind every human activity. The imagination that sparks the fire of the future. The catalyst for change.

The Entrepreneur lives in the future, never in the past, rarely in the present. He's happiest when left free to construct images of "what-if" and "if-when."

In science, the entrepreneurial personality works in the most abstract and least pragmatic areas of particle physics, pure mathematics, and theoretical astronomy. In art, it thrives in the rarified arena of the avant garde. In business, The Entrepreneur is the innovator, the grand strategist, the creator of new methods for penetrating or creating new markets, the world-bending giant—like Sears and Roebuck, Henry Ford, Tom Watson of IBM and Ray Kroc of McDonald's.

The Entrepreneur is our creative personality; always at its best dealing with the unknown, prodding the future, creating probabilities out of possibilities, engineering chaos into harmony.

Every strong entrepreneurial personality has an extraordinary need for control. Living as he does in the visionary world of the future, he needs control of people and events in the present so that he can concentrate on his dreams.

Given his need for change, The Entrepreneur creates a great deal of havoc around him which is predictably unsettling for those he enlists in his projects. As a result, he often finds himself rapidly outdistancing the others. The farther ahead he is, the greater the effort required to pull his cohorts along. This then becomes the entrepreneurial world-view: A world made up of both an overabundance of opportunities and dragging feet.

The problem is, how can he pursue the opportunities without getting mired down by the feet? The way he usually chooses is to bully, harass, excoriate, flatter, cajole, scream, and finally, when all else fails, promise whatever he must to keep the project moving.

To The Entrepreneur, "ordinary man" is always a problem that gets in the way of the dream.

The Manager

The managerial personality is pragmatic. Without The Manager there would be no planning, no order, no predictability.

The Manager is the part of us that goes to Sears and buys stacking plastic boxes, takes them back to the garage, and systematically stores all the various sized nuts, bolts, and screws in their own carefully identified drawer. He then hangs all of the tools in impeccable order on the walls (lawn tools on one wall, carpentry tools on another) and, to be absolutely certain that order is not disturbed, paints a picture of each tool on the wall where it hangs!

If The Entrepreneur lives in the future, The Manager lives in the past. Where The Entrepreneur craves control, The Manager craves order. Where The Entrepreneur thrives on change, The Manager compulsively clings to the status quo. Where The Entrepreneur invariably sees the opportunity in events, The Manager invariably sees the problems.

The Manager builds a house and then lives in it, forever. The Entrepreneur builds a house and the instant it's done begins planning the next one.

The Manager creates neat, orderly rows of things. The Entrepreneur creates the things The Manager puts in rows. The Manager is the one who runs after The Entrepreneur to clean up the mess. Without The Entrepreneur there would be no mess to clean up.

Without The Manager, there could be no business, no society. Without The Entrepreneur, there would be no innovation. It is the tension between The Entrepreneur's vision and The Manager's pragmatism that creates the synthesis from which all great works are born.

The Technician

The Technician is the doer. "If you want it done right, do it yourself" is The Technicians' credo. The Technician loves to tinker. Things are to be taken apart and put back together again. Things aren't supposed to be dreamed about, they're supposed to be done.

If The Entrepreneur lives in the future and The Manager in the past, The Technician lives in the present. He loves the feel of things and the fact that things *can* get done. As long as The Technician is working, he is happy, but only on one thing at a time. He knows that two things can't get done simultaneously; only a fool would try. So he works steadily and is happiest when he is in control of the work flow. As a result, The Technician mistrusts those he works for, because they are always trying to get more work done than is either possible or necessary.

To The Technician, thinking is unproductive unless it's thinking about the work that needs to be done. As a result, he is suspicious of lofty ideas or abstractions. Thinking isn't work, it gets in the way of work. He's not interested in ideas, he's interested in how-to-do-it. All ideas need to be reduced to methodology if they are to be of any value. And with good reason. The Technician knows that if it weren't for him, the world would be in more trouble than it already is. Nothing would get done, but lots of people would be *thinking* about it.

18

Put another way, The Entrepreneur dreams, The Manager frets, and The Technician ruminates.

The Technician is a resolute individualist, standing his ground, producing today's bread to eat at tonight's dinner. He is the backbone of every cultural tradition, but most importantly of ours. If he didn't do it, it wouldn't get done.

Everyone gets in The Technician's way. The Entrepreneur is always throwing a monkeywrench into his day with the creation of yet another "great new idea." On the other hand, The Entrepreneur is always creating new and interesting work for The Technician to do, thus establishing a potentially symbiotic relationship. Unfortunately, it rarely works out that way. Since most entrepreneurial ideas *don't* work in the real world, The Technician's usual experience is one of frustration and annoyance at being interrupted in the course of doing what *needs* to be done to try something new that probably doesn't need to be done at all.

The Manager is also a problem to The Technician because he is determined to impose order on The Technician's work, to reduce him to a part of "the system." But being a rugged individualist, The Technician can't stand being treated that way. To The Technician, "the system" is dehumanizing, cold, antiseptic, and impersonal. It violates his individuality. Work is what a *person* does. And to the degree that it's not, work becomes something foreign. To The Manager, however, work is a system of results in which The Technician is but a component part.

To The Manager, then, The Technician becomes a problem to be managed. To The Technician, The Manager becomes a meddler to be avoided. To both of them, The Entrepreneur is the one who got them into trouble in the first place!

■ ■

The fact of the matter is that we all have an Entrepreneur, Manager, and Technician inside us. And if they were equally balanced, we'd be describing an incredibly competent individual.

The Entrepreneur would be free to forge ahead into new areas of interest; The Manager would be solidifying the base of operations; and The Technician would be doing the technical work. Each would derive satisfaction from the work he does best, serving the whole in the most productive way. Unfortunately, our experience shows us that few people who go into business are blessed with such a balance. Instead, the typical small business owner is only 10 percent Entrepreneur, 20 percent Manager and 70 percent Technician.

The Entrepreneur wakes up with a vision. The Manager screams "Oh, no!" And while the two are battling it out, The Technician seizes the opportunity to go into business for himself. Not to pursue the entrepreneurial dream, however, *but to finally wrest control of his work from the other two.*

To The Technician it's a dream come true. The Boss is dead. But to the business it's a disaster, because the wrong person is at the helm. The Technician is in charge!

3

INFANCY: THE
ENTREPRENEURIAL PHASE

"... my Uncle Sol had a skunk farm but the skunks caught
cold and died and so my Uncle Sol imitated the skunks in a
subtle manner ..."

e. e. cummings
Collected Poems

It is self-evident that businesses, like people, are supposed
to grow; and with growth, comes change. Unfortunately,
most businesses are not run by this principle. Most businesses are operated instead according to what the *owner*
wants as opposed to what the *business* needs. And what
The Technician who runs the company wants is not
growth or change, but exactly the opposite. He wants a
place to go to work, free to do what he wants, when he
wants, free from the constraints of working for The Boss.
Unfortunately, what The Technician wants dooms his
business before it even begins.

To understand why, let's take a look at the three
phases of a business's growth: Infancy, Adolescence, and
Maturity. Understanding each phase, and what goes on in
the business owner's mind during each of them, is critical

to discovering why most businesses don't succeed while ensuring that yours does.

■ ■

The Boss is dead, and you, The Technician, are free at last. Finally, you can do your own thing in your own business. Hope runs high. The air is electric with possibility. It's like being let out of school for the summer. Your new-found freedom is intoxicating.

In the beginning nothing is too much for your business to ask. As The Technician, you're accustomed to "paying your dues." So the hours devoted to the business during Infancy are not spent grudgingly, but optimistically. There's work to be done, and that's what you're all about. After all, your middle name is Work. "Besides," you think, "this work is for *me*."

And so you work. Ten, twelve, fourteen hours a day. Seven days a week. Even when you're at home, you're at work. All your thoughts, all your feelings, revolve around your new business. You can't get it out of your mind. You're consumed by it; totally invested in doing whatever is necessary to keep it alive.

But now you're doing not only the work you *know* how to do, but the work you *don't* know how to do as well. You're not only making it; but you're also buying it, selling it, and shipping it. During Infancy, you're a Master Juggler, keeping all the balls in the air.

It's easy to spot a business in Infancy—*the owner and the business are one and the same thing*. If you removed the owner from an Infancy business, there would be no business left. It would disappear! In Infancy, you *are* the business. It's even named after you—"SAM'S PLACE," "TOMMY'S JOINT," "MARY'S FINE FOODS"—so the customer won't forget that you're the boss.

And soon—if you're lucky—all of the sweat, worry, and work begin to pay off. You're good. You work hard. The customers don't forget. They're coming back. They're sending in friends. Their friends have friends. And they're all talking about Sam, Tommy, and Mary. They're all talking about you.

If you can believe what your customers are saying, there's never been anyone like Sam, Tommy, and Mary. Sam, Tommy, and Mary are just like old friends. They work hard for their money. And they do good work. Sam is the best barber I ever went to. Tommy is the best printer I ever used. Mary makes the best corned beef sandwich I ever ate. Your customers are *crazy* about you. They keep coming, in droves.

And you love it!

But then it changes. Subtly at first, but gradually it becomes obvious. You're falling behind. There's more work to do than you can possibly get done. The customers are relentless. They want you, they need you. You've spoiled them for anyone else. You're working at breakneck speed. And then the inevitable happens.

You, the Master Juggler, begin to drop some of the balls!

It can't be helped. No matter how hard you try, you simply can't catch them all. Your enthusiasm for working with the customers wanes. Deliveries, once early, are now late. The product begins to show the wear and tear. Nothing seems to work the way it did at first.

Sam's haircuts don't look the way they used to. "I said short in the back, not on the sides." "My name's not Fred; that's my brother—and I never had a crewcut!"

Glitches start showing up in Tommy's printing: typos, ink smudges, wrong colors, wrong paper. "I didn't order business cards, I ordered catalog covers." "Pink? I said brown!"

Mary's best-tasting-biggest-stack-of-corned-beef-in-the-world suddenly looks like pastrami. It *is* pastrami. "Didn't you ask for pastrami?" Another irritated voice calls out: "Where's my pastrami sandwich? This is corned beef!" And yet another, "What are these garbanzo beans doing in my meatloaf?"

What do you do? You stretch. You work harder. You put in more time, more energy. If you put in twelve hours before, you now put in fourteen. If you put in fourteen hours before, you now put in sixteen. If you put in sixteen hours before, you now put in twenty. But the balls keep dropping!

All of a sudden, Sam, Tommy, and Mary wish their names weren't on the sign. All of a sudden, they want to hide. All of a sudden, you find yourself at the end of an unbelievably hectic week, late on a Saturday night, pouring over the books, trying to make some sense out of the mess, thinking about all of the work you didn't get done this week, and all of the work waiting for you next week. And you suddenly realize *it simply isn't going to get done.* There's simply no way in the world you can do all that work yourself!

In a flash, you realize that your business has become the Boss you thought you left behind. *There's no getting rid of the Boss!*

Infancy ends when the owner realizes that the business cannot continue to run the way it has been; that, in order for it to survive, it will have to change. When that happens—when the reality sinks in—most business failures occur. When that happens, most of The Technicians lock their doors behind them and walk away.

The rest go on to Adolescence.

4

ADOLESCENCE:
GETTING SOME HELP

"As governments, we stumble from crisis to crash program, lurching into the future without plan, without hope, without vision."

Alvin Toffler
The Third Wave

Adolescence begins at the point in the life of your business when you decide to get some help. There's no telling how soon this will happen. But it *always* happens, precipitated by a crisis in the Infancy stage. Every business that lasts must grow into the Adolescent phase.

What kind of help do you, the overloaded Technician, go out to get? The answer is as easy as it is inevitable: *technical help.* Someone with experience. Someone with experience in your kind of business. Someone who knows how to do the technical work that isn't getting done—usually the work you don't like to do.

The sales-oriented owner goes out to find a production person. The production-oriented owner looks for a sales person. And just about everybody tries to find someone to do the books!

And so it is that you bring in your first employee—

Harry, a 68-year-old bookkeeper who's been doing the books since he was twelve years old, in the Old Country. Harry knows the books. He knows how to do the books in eight different languages. But most important, Harry has twenty-two years of experience doing the books in a company *just like yours.* There is nothing Harry doesn't know about your kind of business. And now he's yours. The world suddenly looks brighter again. A major ball is about to be caught—and by somebody else for a change!

It's Monday morning. Harry arrives. You greet him warmly and, let's face it, feverishly. You've spent all weekend getting ready for this moment. You cleared out a generous space for him. You arranged the books and the stack of unopened letters on his desk. You bought a coffee cup with "Harry" printed on it. You were even thoughtful enough to find a cushion for his chair (he'll be sitting for a long time).

There's a critical moment in every business when the owner hires his very first employee to do the work he doesn't know how to do himself, or doesn't want to do. In your business, Harry is that person. And this Monday morning is that critical time.

Think about it.

You've taken a big step. The books are on Harry's desk now. He's about to become the only other person in the whole world who knows the real story about you and your business. He's going to take one look at the books and know the truth. He's going to know that *you don't know what you're doing.*

The question is, what's he going to do about it? Will he laugh? Will he leave? Or will he go to work? If Harry won't do the books, who will?

Suddenly, you hear the quiet, systematic clattering of the calculator's keys from Harry's desk. He's working!

Harry's going to stay! You can't believe your luck. You're not going to have to do the books anymore. You understand, in a single stroke, what it means to be in business in a way you never understood before.

"I don't have to do that anymore!"

At last you're free. The instant you hand over a job to somebody else, The Manager in you wakes up and The Technician temporarily goes to sleep. Your worries are over. Someone else is going to do that now.

But at the same time—unaccustomed as you are to being The Manager—your newfound freedom takes on an all too common form. Management by *abdication* rather than by *delegation*. In short, you give Harry the books and run.

And for a while you *are* free, relatively at least. You still have all the other work to do. But when Harry's not totally immersed in the books, you get him to answer the phone. And when he's not answering the phone, you get him to do a little shipping and receiving. And when he's not doing the shipping and receiving, he might as well handle a few customers. And when he's not handling a few customers, well, who knows what you could think of next?

Life becomes easier. You begin to take a little longer lunch: thirty minutes instead of fifteen. You leave a little earlier at the end of the day; eight o'clock instead of nine. Harry comes to you occasionally to tell you what he needs, and you, busy as usual, simply tell him to handle it. *How* doesn't matter. Just don't bother you with the details.

Harry needs more people. The business is beginning to grow. Busy as usual, you tell him to hire them. He does. Harry's a wonder. It's great to have a guy like Harry. You don't have to think about what he's doing; you don't have to worry about how he's getting along. He never complains. He just works. And he's doing all the work you hate to do. It's the best of all possible worlds. You get to be the boss, doing the work you love to do, and Harry takes care of everything else.

And then it happens.

A customer calls to complain about the shabby treatment she received from one of your people. "Who was it?" She doesn't know, but if you're going to hire people like that she'll take her business elsewhere.

You promise to look into it.

Your banker calls to tell you that you're overdrawn. "How did that happen?" you ask him. He doesn't know, but if you don't watch it more closely he'll have to "take steps."

You promise to look into it.

Your oldest supplier calls to tell you that the order you placed the week before was placed wrong, so the shipment will be ten weeks late. What's more, *you're* going to have to eat the overage. "How did that happen?" you ask him. He doesn't know, but if you can't manage your ordering better than that, he'll have to look at other options.

You promise to look into it.

Out on the shipping dock, you walk up to a kid Harry hired. He's wrapping a package. You look at the package and explode. "Who taught you to wrap a package like this?" you ask the surprised kid. "Didn't anyone show you how to do this right? Here, give it to me, I'll do it myself."

And you do.

That very afternoon, you happen to be walking by the production line. You almost drop in your tracks. "Who taught you to do it that way?," you stammer to the shocked production person. "Didn't anybody show you how to do it right? Here, give it to me, I'll do it myself."

And you do.

The very next morning, you're talking to the new salesperson, also hired by Harry. "What's happening to customer A?" you ask her. Her answer sends you into a rage. "When *I* took care of him we never had problems like that! Here, give it to me, I'll take care of it myself."

And you do.

And the young shipping clerk looks at the production person, they both look at the new salesperson, and they all look at Harry, who's their Acting Boss, and ask: "Who the hell was *that?*" Harry just shrugs and says (as only a man who's worked for other people for fifty-plus years can say): "Oh, that was just the boss."

What Harry knows is something you're about to learn. It's only the beginning. It's the beginning of a process which occurs in *every* Adolescent business, once the owner's Management by Abdication begins to take its toll. It's the beginning of a process of deterioration, in which the number of balls in the air not only exceeds *your* ability to juggle them effectively, but your *people's* ability as well.

The balls begin to fall, faster and with greater confusion than they ever did when you were doing everything yourself. And as the thud of their landings becomes deafening, you begin to realize that you never should have trusted Harry. You never should have trusted *anyone*. You should have known better.

You begin to realize that no one cares about your business the way you do. No one is willing to work as hard as you work. No one has your judgment, or your ability, or your desire, or your interest. If it's going to get done, *you're* the one who's going to have to do it.

So you run back into your business to become the Master Juggler again. It's the same old story. One finds the owner of every Adolescent business doing, doing, doing— doing the work of the business—*despite the fact that he*

29

now has people who are supposed to be doing it for him.

And the more *he* does, the less *they* do. And the less they do the more he knows that if it's going to get done, he's going to have to do it himself. So he interferes with what they have to do all the more.

But Harry knew this when he started. He could have told you—his new boss—that ultimately the Boss *always* interferes. That the work will *never* be done to the Boss's satisfaction. And the reason is that the Boss always changes his mind about what needs to be done, and how.

What Harry doesn't know, however, is why—why you're such a madman.

It's not your people. It's not the complaining customer. It's not the banker, or the vendor, or the incorrectly wrapped package. It's not that "nobody cares," or that "nothing gets done on time."

No, it's not the *world* that's the problem. *It's that you simply don't know how to do it any other way.* For you to act differently you would need a totally new set of skills; the skills of The Manager and the skills of The Entrepreneur.

But The Technician in you won't stop long enough for that to happen. The resulting chaos is nothing more than a direct consequence of The Technician's inability to change as fast as your business demands.

You've reached the limits of your Comfort Zone.

5

BEYOND
THE COMFORT ZONE

"Drastic change creates an estrangement from the self, and generates a need for a new birth of a new identity. And it perhaps depends on the way this need is satisfied whether the process of change runs smoothly or is attended with convulsions and explosions."

Eric Hoffer
The Temper of our Time

Every Adolescent business reaches a point where it pushes beyond its owner's Comfort Zone—the boundary within which he feels secure in his ability to control his environment, and outside of which he begins to lose that control.

The Technician's boundary is determined by how much he can do himself. The Manager's is defined by how many technicians he can supervise effectively or how many subordinate managers he can organize into a productive effort. The Entrepreneur's boundary is a function of how many managers he can engage in pursuit of his vision.

As a business grows, it invariably exceeds its owner's ability to control it—to touch, feel, and see the work that needs to be done, and to inspect its progress personally as every technician needs to do. Out of desperation, he does what he knows how to do rather than what he doesn't, thereby abdicating his role as manager and passing his accountability down to someone else—a "Harry."

At that point, his desperation turns into hope. He hopes that Harry will handle it so that he won't have to worry about it anymore.

But Harry has needs of his own. Harry's also a technician. He needs more direction than The Technician can give him. He needs to know why he's doing what he's doing. He needs to know the result he's accountable for and the standards against which his work is being evaluated. He also needs to know where the business is going and where his accountabilities fit into its overall strategy.

To produce effectively, Harry needs something the owner isn't capable of giving him—a manager! And the lack of one causes the business to go into a tailspin.

And as the business grows beyond the owner's Comfort Zone—as the tailspin accelerates—there are only three courses of action to be taken, only three ways the business can turn. It can return to Infancy. It can go for broke. Or it can hang on for dear life.

Let's take a look at each.

Getting Small Again

One of the most consistent and predictable reactions of The Technician-turned-business-owner to Adolescent chaos is the decision to "get small" again. If you can't control the chaos, get rid of it. Go back to the way it used to be when you did everything yourself, when you didn't have people to worry about, or too many customers, or too many unpayable payables and unreceivable receivables, or too much inventory.

In short, go back to the time when business was simple, back to Infancy.

And thousands upon thousands of technicians do just that. They get rid of their people, get rid of their inventory, wrap up their payables in a large bag, rent a smaller facility, put the machine in the middle, put the telephone by the machine, and go back to doing it all by themselves again.

They go back to being the owner, sole proprietor, chief cook and bottle washer—doing everything that needs to be done, all alone, but comfortable with the feeling of re-gained control.

"What can go wrong?" they think to themselves, for-getting at once that they've been there before. Predictably, this too takes its toll.

One morning—it could be six weeks or six years fol-lowing the day you "got small" again—the inevitable hap-pens. You wake up in bed, and your spouse turns to you and says: "What's wrong? You're not looking too good." "I'm not feeling too good," you answer. "Do you want to talk about it?" he or she asks. "It's simple," you say, "I don't want to go in there anymore!"

Then your spouse asks you the obvious question "But if *you* don't, who will?"

And all of a sudden you are struck with the reality of your condition. You realize something you've avoided all these years. You come face to face with the unavoidable truth:

You don't own a *business*, you own a *job!*

What's more, it's the worst job in the world! You can't close it when you want to, because if it's closed you don't get paid. You can't leave it when you want to, because when you leave there's nobody there to do the work. You can't sell it when you want to, because who wants to buy a job?

At that point you feel the despair and the cynicism. If

there was ever a dream, however small, it's gone. And with it, any desire to keep busy, busy, busy. You don't wash the windows anymore. You don't sweep the floors. The customers become a problem rather than an opportunity, because if somebody buys something *you're* going to have to do the work. Your standards of dress deteriorate. The sign on the front door fades and peels. And you don't care. For when the dream is gone, the only thing left is work. The tyranny of routine. The day-to-day grind of purposeless activity.

Finally, you close the doors. There's nothing to keep you there anymore.

According to the Small Business Administration, more than 400,000 such businesses close their doors in this country every year. It's understandable. Your business, once the shining promise of your life, and now no promise at all, has gradually become a mortuary for dead dreams.

Going for Broke

The Adolescent business has another alternative that is certainly less painful and decidedly more dramatic than "getting small." It can just keep growing faster and faster until it self-destructs of its own momentum.

The roll call is endless: Itel, Osbourne Computer, Coleco and countless more. All such "going-for-broke" companies were started with an Entrepreneurial Seizure by a technician who focused on the wrong end of the business, the commodity the business made, rather than the business itself.

"Going-for-broke" businesses are a sign of our time. They are a high-tech phenomenon. With the explosion of new technology and the numbers of those who create it, a whole new breed of technicians has flocked to the business arena. Along with these wizards and their seemingly unlimited technical virtuosity, an avalanche of new products has thundered through the wide-open doors of an enthralled and receptive marketplace. Unfortunately, most of these companies barely get through the doors before the uncontrollable momentum that got them there forces them to stumble and then fall.

All the excesses of Adolescence, frustrating and bewildering as they might be in a normally expanding company, are disastrous in a "going-for-broke" business. As quickly as it grows, chaos grows even faster. For tied to the tail of a technological breakthrough, The Technician and his people rarely break free long enough to gain some perspective about their condition. The demand for the commodity of which they are so proud quickly exceeds their chronically Adolescent ability to produce it.

The result is almost always catastrophic. The business explodes, leaving behind it people who most often justify the explosion as an inevitable consequence of doing business on a "fast track" where luck and speed and a brilliant bit of technological derring-do are the necessary components for making it big.

The reality is otherwise.

Luck and speed and brilliant technology have never been enough, because somebody is always luckier, faster, and technologically brighter. Unfortunately, once on a fast track, there's precious little time to listen. The race is won by reflex, a stroke of genius, or a stroke of luck.

"Going for broke" is the high-tech equivalent of Russian Roulette, oftentimes played by people who don't even know the gun is loaded!

Hanging in There

The most tragic possibility of all for an Adolescent business is that it stays in business—it actually survives!

You're an incredibly strong-willed, stubborn, single-minded son-of-a-bitch who's determined not to be beaten. You go into your business every morning with a vengeance, absolutely convinced that it's a jungle out there, and fully committed to doing whatever's necessary to survive.

And you *do* survive. Kicking and scratching, beating up your people and your customers, ranting and raving at your family and friends—becaue, after all, you've got to keep the business going. And you only know one way to do that. *You must be there, all the time.*

You're *consumed* by the business and the possibility of losing it. And so you put everything you have into it. For whatever reason, you manage to keep it going. Day after day, fighting the same battles, in exactly the same way you did the day before. You never change. Night after night, you go home to unwind, only to wind up even tighter in anticipation of tomorrow.

Finally, your *business* doesn't explode—you do!

You're like a twelve cylinder engine working on one cylinder, pumping away, trying with everything you have to produce twelve cylinders' worth of results. Finally, there's nothing left. There's simply nothing more you can do, except face the fact that one cylinder can't produce twelve cylinders' worth of results, no matter how hard it tries. Something has to give, and that something is you.

Does it all sound familiar? If you've been in business, it should. If you haven't, it probably will because the condition of Infancy and Adolescence dominates American business.

It is the condition of 99 percent of the businesses we've visited over the past ten years, a condition of rampant confusion and tragically wasted lives.

There's got to be a better way.

6

MATURITY AND THE ENTREPRENEURIAL PERSPECTIVE

"They see the pattern, understand the order, experience the vision."

Peter Drucker
The New Society

Maturity, the third phase of a company's growth, is exemplified by the best businesses in the world. Businesses such as IBM, McDonald's, and Procter & Gamble. A Mature business knows how it got to be where it is, and what it must do to get where it wants to go.

But Maturity is not an inevitable result of the first two phases. It is not the end product of a serial process, beginning with Infancy and moving through Adolescence. No, IBM, McDonald's and Procter & Gamble didn't *end up* as Mature companies. They *started out* that way! The people who started them had a totally different perspective about what a business is and why it works.

The person who launches his business as a Mature company must also go through Infancy and Adolescence. He simply goes through them in an entirely different way.

It's his *perspective* that makes the difference.

The Entrepreneurial Perspective

I once heard a story about Tom Watson, the founder of IBM. Asked to what he attributed the phenomenal success of IBM, he is said to have answered:

IBM is what it is today for three special reasons. The first reason is that, at the very beginning, I had a very clear picture of what the company would look like when it was finally done. You might say I had a model in my mind of what it would look like when the dream—my vision—was in place.

The second reason was that once I had that picture, I then asked myself how a company which looked like that would have to act. I then created a picture of how IBM would act when it was finally done.

The third reason IBM has been so successful was that once I had a picture of how IBM would look when the dream was in place and how such a company would have to act, I then realized that, unless we began to act that way from the very beginning, we would never get there.

In other words, I realized that for IBM to become a great company it would have to act like a great company long before it ever became one.

From the very outset, IBM was fashioned after the template of my vision. And each and every day we attempted to model the company after that template. At the end of each day, we asked ourselves how well we did, discovered the disparity between where we were and where we had committed ourselves to be, and, at the start of the following day, set out to make up for the difference.

Every day at IBM was a day devoted to business development, *not* doing business.

We didn't do *business at IBM, we* built *one.*

My storyteller may not have had Watson's words exactly verbatim, but what the story tells us is very important. It reveals an understanding of what makes a great business great. It also tells us what makes all other businesses survivable at their best; intolerable at their worst.

It tells us that the very best businesses are fashioned after a model of a business that works.

Understanding this and acting upon it is the Entrepreneurial Perspective, which says it's not the commodity or the work itself that is important. What's important is the *business:* how it looks, how it acts, how it does what it is intended to do.

Unfortunately, most people who go into business don't have a model of a *business* that works, *but of work itself.* That is the Technician's Perspective, which differs from the Entrepreneurial Perspective in the following ways:

- The Entrepreneurial Perspective asks the question: "How must the business work?" The Technician's Perspective asks: "What work has to be done?"

- The Entrepreneurial Perspective sees the business as a system for producing *outside* results—for the customer—resulting in profits. The Technician's Perspective sees the business as a place in which people work to produce *inside* results—for The Technician —producing income.

- The Entrepreneurial Perspective starts with a picture of a well-defined future, and then comes back to the present with the intention of changing it to match the vision. The Technician's Perspective starts with the present, and then looks forward to an uncertain future with the hope of keeping it much like the present.

• The Entrepreneurial Perspective envisions the business in its entirety, from which is derived its parts. The Technician's Perspective envisions the business in parts, from which is constructed the whole.

• The Entrepreneurial Perspective is an integrated vision of the world. The Technician's Perspective is a fragmented vision of the world.

• To The Entrepreneur, the present-day world is modeled after his vision. To The Technician, the future is modeled after the present-day world.

Is it any wonder that the Entrepreneurial Perspective is absolutely necessary for the creation of a great business, while the Technician's produces its exact opposite?

The Entrepreneurial Perspective adopts a wider, more expansive scale. It views the business as a network of components, each contributing to some larger pattern that comes together in such a way as to produce a specifically planned result.

Each step in the development of such a business is measurable, if not quantitatively, at least, qualitatively. There's a standard for the business, a form, a way of being that can be translated into things to do today that best exemplify it. The business operates according to articulated rules and principles. It has a clear, recognizable form.

With the Technician's Perspective, however, the scale is narrower, more inhibited, confined principally to the work being done. As a result, The Technician's business becomes increasingly oppressive, less exhilarating, closed off from the larger world outside. His business, therefore, is reduced to steps that fail to take him anywhere other than to the next step, itself nothing more than a replica of the one before it. Routine becomes the order of the day. Work is done for work's sake alone, forsaking any higher purpose, any meaning for what needs to be done other than the need to just do it.

The Technician sees no connection between where his business is going and where it is now.

Lacking the grander scale and visionary guidance manifest in the Entrepreneurial Model, The Technician is left to construct a model each step of the way. But the only model from which to construct it is the model of past experience, the model of work. *Exactly the opposite* of what he needs if the business is to free him of the work he's grown accustomed to doing.

The Entrepreneurial Model

What does The Entrepreneur see off in the distance that The Technician finds so difficult to see? What exactly is the Entrepreneurial Model?

It's a model of a business that fulfills the perceived needs of a specific segment of consumers in an innovative way.

The Entrepreneurial Model looks at a business as if it were a product, sitting on a shelf and competing for the consumer's attention against a whole shelf of competing products (or businesses).

Said another way, the Entrepreneurial Model has less

to do with *what's* done in a business, and more to do with *how* it's done.

When The Entrepreneur creates the model, he surveys the world and asks: "Where is the opportunity?" Having identified it, he then goes back to the drawing board and constructs a solution to the frustrations he finds among a certain group of consumers. A solution in the form of a business that looks and acts in a very specific way, the way the *consumer* needs it to look and act, *not* The Entrepreneur.

"How will my business look to the consumer?" The Entrepreneur asks. "How will my business stand out from all the rest?"

Thus, the Entrepreneurial Model does not start with a picture of the *business* to be created, but of the *customer* for whom the business is to be created. It understands that *without a clear picture of that customer, no business can succeed.*

The Technician, on the other hand, looks inwardly to define his skills, and only looks outwardly to ask, "How can I sell them?" The result is a business that almost inevitably focuses on the thing it sells rather than the way the business goes about it or the customer to whom it's to be sold. The business is designed to satisfy The Technician who created it, not the consumer.

To The Entrepreneur, the *business* is the product. As far as The Technician is concerned, the product is what he delivers to the consumer. So the consumer is always a problem for The Technician because the consumer never seems to want what he has to offer. To The Entrepreneur, however, the customer is always an opportunity because within the customer is a continuing parade of wants begging to be satisfied. All The Entrepreneur has to do is find out what they are. As a result, the world is a continuing surprise, a treasure hunt. To The Technician, the world is a place that never seems to let him do what he wants to do; it rarely applauds his efforts.

The question then becomes, how can we introduce the Entrepreneurial Model to The Technician in such a way that he can understand it and utilize it?

The answer is, we can't. The Technician isn't interested.

What we must do, instead, is to give the undeveloped Entrepreneur in each of us the information he needs to grow, to expand sufficiently beyond the limitations of The Technician's Comfort Zone so as to experience a vision of a business that works.

What we must do is provide our entrepreneur with a model of business that works, a model that is so exciting that it stimulates our entrepreneurial personality—our creative side—to break out of our technician's bounds once and for all; a model that sparks the entrepreneurial imagination in each of us with such a resounding shock that by the time The Technician wakes up to the fact it will be too late. The Entrepreneur will be well on his way.

But if this is to work, The Manager and The Technician need their own Models. If The Entrepreneur drives the business, The Manager must make certain it has the necessary fuel and that the engine and chassis are in a good state of repair. The Technician, on the other hand, must find work to do that satisfies his need for direct interaction with every nut and bolt.

In short, the Model must be balanced and inclusive if it is to work.

To find such a model, let us examine a revolutionary development that has transformed American business in an astonishing way—The Turn-Key Revolution.

The Turn-Key Revolution: A New View of Business

The Turn-Key Revolution: A New View of Business

7

THE TURN-KEY REVOLUTION

"Systems theory looks at the world in terms of the inter-relatedness of all phenomena, and in this framework an integrated whole whose properties cannot be reduced to those of its parts is called a system."

Fritjof Capra
The Turning Point

The Industrial Revolution, the Technological Revolution, the Information Explosion are all familiar phenomena in today's world. There is no question of the impact each has had on our lives.

If asked to describe the Turn-Key Revolution, however, most people would simply respond with a blank stare. Yet its impact on American business, and the inferences we can draw about that impact for the future, are as profound as any of the phenomena cited above.

For at the heart of the Turn-Key Revolution is a way of doing business that has the power to dramatically transform any company from a condition of chaos to a condition of order, excitement, and continuous growth. I'm talking about the key to the development of a successful business: the ultimately balanced Model of a business that works.

The Franchise Phenomenon

It all started in 1952 when a 52-year old salesman walked into a hamburger stand in San Bernardino, California to sell the two brothers who owned it a milkshake machine.

What he saw there was a miracle.

At least that's how Ray Kroc, the milkshake machine salesman, might have described it. For he had never seen anything like that very first MacDonald's (later to become *Mc*Donald's) hamburger stand.

It worked like a Swiss watch!

Hamburgers were produced in a way he'd never seen before—quickly, efficiently, inexpensively, and identically. Best of all, *anyone* could do it. He watched high school kids working with precision under the supervision of the owners, happily responding to the long lines of customers queued up in front of the stand.

It became apparent to Ray Kroc that what the MacDonald brothers had created was not just another hamburger stand, but a money machine!

Soon after that first visit, Ray Kroc convinced Mac and Jim MacDonald to let him franchise their method. Twelve years and several million hamburgers later, he bought them out and went on to create the largest retail prepared food distribution system in the world.

The success of McDonald's is truly staggering. In less than thirty years, Ray Kroc's McDonald's has become an $8 billion a year business, with more than 8,000 franchise outlets spread throughout the world, serving food to nine million customers *each and every day*. The average McDonald's restaurant produces more than $1 million in annual sales, and is more profitable than almost any other retail business in the world.

But Ray Kroc created much more than just a fantastically successful business. He created the model upon which an entire generation of entrepreneurs have since built their fortunes: the franchise phenomenon.

It started as a trickle when a few entrepreneurs began to experiment with Kroc's formula for success. But it wasn't long before the trickle turned into Niagara Falls! Indeed, by 1984, franchising had produced more than *500,-000 businesses* nationwide, selling everything from hamburgers to legal services.

In 1984 alone, franchises rang up almost $400 billion in sales—*one out of every three retail dollars spent in the nation*—and had more than 4.5 million full- and part-time employees. Franchises had become the largest employer of high school youth in the country's economy.

But the genius of McDonald's isn't franchising itself. The franchise has been around for more than a hundred years. Many companies—Coca-Cola and General Motors among them—have utilized franchising as an effective method of distribution to reach broadly expanding markets inexpensively. The true genius of Ray Kroc's McDonald's is the Business Format Franchise.

It is the Business Format Franchise that has revolutionized American business. It is the Business Format Franchise, growing at an average of 8,000 new outlets every year, that has spawned so much of the success of the franchise phenomenon over the past thirty years. And it is the Business Format Franchise that is the key to an understanding of the Turn-Key Revolution, and with it, the future success of your business.

Turning the Key: The Business Format Franchise

The early franchising businesses, many of which still exist, were called "trade name" franchises. Under this system, the franchisor sells or licenses the right to small companies to market its nationally known products locally.

But the Business Format Franchise moves a step beyond the trade name franchise. The Business Format Franchise not only lends its name to the smaller enterprise *but also provides the franchisee with an entire system of doing business.*

And in that difference lies the true significance of the Turn-Key Revolution and its phenomenal success.

The Turn-Key Revolution and the Business Format Franchise were born of a belief that runs counter to what most business founders in this country believe. Most business founders believe that *the success of a business resides in the success of the product it sells.* To the trade name franchisor, the value of the franchise lies in the value of the brand name which it's licensing: Cadillac, Mercedes, Coca-Cola.

There was a time when that belief was true, but it isn't any more. In a world where brand names proliferate like snowflakes in a Minnesota blizzard, it becomes more and more difficult—and infinitely more expensive—to establish a secure position with a brand name and expect to keep it.

As a result, trade name franchises have been declining over the same period that franchising in general has been exploding. Between 1982 and 1984, the number of trade name franchises dropped at the rate of 1,250 per month while sales of franchises increased at the remarkable rate of 1,500 per month!

It is the Business Format Franchise that has accounted for that growth. Because the Business Format Franchise is built upon the belief that the true product of a business is not *what* it sells but *how* it sells it. *The true product of a business is the business itself.*

What Ray Kroc understood at McDonald's was that the *hamburger* wasn't his product, *McDonald's* was. And he believed that for a most important reason.

Selling the Business Instead of the Product

Ray Kroc was the consummate entrepreneur. And like most entrepreneurs, he suffered from one major liability. He had a huge dream and very little money.

Enter the franchisee.

The franchisee became the vehicle for Ray Kroc to realize his dream.

At that point, Ray Kroc began to look at his business as the product, and at the franchisee as his first, last, and most important customer. For the franchisee wasn't interested in hamburgers or french fries or milkshakes; he was interested in the *business*. Driven by the desire to buy a business, the franchisee only wanted to know one thing: "Does it work?"

Ray Kroc's most important concern then became how to make certain his business would work *better than any other*. If McDonald's was to fulfill the dream he had for it, *the franchisee would have to be willing to buy it*. And the only way Ray Kroc could assure himself of that was to make certain that it worked better than any of the other business products around.

He wasn't competing with other hamburger businesses. He was competing with every other business opportunity!

But there was a second reason that Ray Kroc had for making certain McDonald's would work. Given the failure rate of most small businesses, he must have realized a crucial fact: for McDonald's to be a predictable success, the business would *have to* work because the franchisee, if left to his own devices, most assuredly wouldn't!

Once, he understood this, Ray Kroc's problem became his opportunity. Forced to create a business that worked in order to sell it, he also created a business that would work once it was sold—*no matter who bought it.* Armed with that realization, he set about the task of creating a foolproof, predictable business.

He went to work *on* his business, not *in* it.

He began to think about his business like an engineer working on a pre-production prototype of a mass-produceable product. He began to think about McDonald's just like Henry Ford must have thought about the Model T. How would the components of the prototype have to be constructed so that it could be assembled at very low cost from totally interchangeable parts? How would the components of the prototype have to be constructed so that the resulting business system could be replicated over and over again, each business working—just like the Model T—as reliably as the thousands that preceded it?

What Ray Kroc did was to apply the thinking behind the Industrial Revolution to the process of Business Development, and to a degree never before experienced in a business enterprise.

The business-as-a-product would only sell if it worked. And the only way to make certain it would work in the hands of a franchisee anywhere in the world would be to build it out of perfectly predictable components that could be tested in a prototype long before every going into mass production.

Therein lies the secret behind the stunning success of the Business Format Franchise, the launching pad for the Turn-Key Revolution.

That secret is the Franchise Prototype. It is in the

Franchise Prototype where every successful franchisor builds his future. And it is the Franchise Prototype that represents the Model you need to make your business work.

8

THE FRANCHISE PROTOTYPE

"Precision instruments are designed to achieve an *idea*, dimensional precision, where perfection is impossible. There is no perfectly shaped part of the motorcycle and never will be, but when you come as close as these instruments take you, remarkable things happen, and you go flying across the countryside under a power that would be called magic if it were not so completely rational in every way."

Robert M. Pirsig
Zen and the Art of Motorcycle Maintenance

The success of the Business Format Franchise is without question the most important news in business.

In 1983 Business Format Franchises reported a success rate of 97 percent in contrast to the 50+ percent failure rate of new independently owned businesses that failed that year. Where 80 percent of all businesses fail in the first five years, 96 percent of all Business Format Franchises succeed!

The reason for that success is the Franchise Prototype.

To the franchisor, the Prototype becomes the working model of the dream; it is the dream in microcosm. The Prototype becomes the incubator and the nursery for all creative thought, the station where creativity is nursed by pragmatism to grow into an innovation that works.

The Franchise Prototype is also the place where all assumptions are put to the test to see how well they work before becoming operational in the business. Without it the franchise would be an impossible dream, as chaotic and undisciplined as any business. The Prototype acts as a buffer between hypothesis and action. Putting ideas to the test in the *real* world rather than the world of competing ideas. The only criterion of value becomes the answer to the ultimate question: "Does it work?"

Once having completed his Prototype, the franchisor then turns to the franchisee and says, "Let me show you how it works." And work it does. The system runs the business. The people run the system.

The system becomes the solution to the problems that have beset all businesses and all human organizations since time immemorial. It integrates all the elements required to make a business work. It transforms a business into a machine, driven by the integrity of its parts, all working in concert toward a realized objective. And it works like nothing else before it. With the Prototype as its progenitor.

At McDonald's, every possible detail of the business system was first tested in the Prototype, and then controlled to a degree never before possible in a people-intensive business. The french fries are left in the warming bin for no more than seven minutes to prevent sogginess. A soggy french fry is not a McDonald's french fry. Hamburgers are removed from the hot trays in no more than ten minutes to retain the proper moisture. The frozen meat patties, precisely identical in size and weight, are turned at exactly the same time on the griddle. Pickles are placed by hand in a set pattern that prevents them from sliding out and landing in the customer's lap. Food is served to the customer in 60 seconds or less.

Discipline, standardization, and order are the watchwords. Cleanliness is enforced with meticulous attention to the most seemingly trivial detail. Ray Kroc was determined that the customer would not equate "inexpensive" with "inattentive" or "cheap." Nowhere has a business ever paid so much attention to the little things, to the system that guarantees the customer that his expectations will be fulfilled in exactly the same way each and every time he returns.

Unlike the trade-name franchise before it, Ray Kroc's system leaves the franchisee with as little operating discretion as possible. This is accomplished by sending him through a rigorous training program before ever being allowed to operate the franchise. At McDonald's, they call it the University of Hamburgerology, or Hamburger U. There, the franchisee learns not how to make hamburgers, but how to run the *system* that makes hamburgers—the system by which McDonald's satisfies its customers every single time. The system that is the foundation of McDonald's uncommon success.

Once the franchisee learns the system, he is given the key to his own business. Thus the name, Turn-Key operation.

The franchisee buys the business, learns how to run it, and then "turns the key." The business does the rest. And the franchisee loves it! If the franchisor has designed the business well, every problem has been thought through. All that's left for the franchisee to do is learn how to manage the system.

That's what the Franchise Prototype is all about. It's a place to conceive and perfect the system. To find out what works because you've worked it. The system isn't something you *bring to* the business. It's something you *derive from* the process of building the business. The Franchise Prototype is the answer to the perpetual question: "How do I give my customer what he wants, while at the same time maintain control of the business that's giving it to him?"

To The Entrepreneur, the Franchise Prototype is the medium through which his vision takes form in the real world. To The Manager, it provides the order, the predictability, the *system* so important to his life. To The Technician, the Prototype is a place in which he is free to do the things he loves to do—technical work. And to the small business owner, therefore, the Franchise Prototype provides the means through which he can finally feed his three personalities in a balanced way while creating a business that works.

So if the Franchise Prototype *is* the answer . . . if it is the balanced Model that will satisfy The Entrepreneur, The Manager, and The Technician all at once, how do you make it work for *you?* How do you put the Franchise Prototype to work in *your* business?

How do *you* build a business that works predictably, effortlessly, and profitably each and every day?

9

WORKING *ON* YOUR BUSINESS, NOT *IN* IT

". . . form is only a beginning. It is the combination of feelings and a function; shapes and things that come to one in connection with the discoveries made as one goes into the wood that pull it together and give meaning to form."

James Krenov
A Cabinetmaker's Notebook

It is critical that you understand the point I'm about to make. For if you do, neither your business nor your life will ever be the same.

The point is: *your business is not your life.* Your business and your life are totally separate things. Your business is something apart from you, with its own needs, its own rules, and its own purposes. An organism, you might say, that will live or die according to how well it performs its sole function: to find and keep customers.

Once you recognize that your life is not your business, but something your business must serve, you can begin to go to work *on* your business, rather than *in* it. This is where you can put the Franchise Prototype to work for you. Where working *on* your business rather than *in* your business will become the central theme of your daily activity, the prime catalyst for everything you do from this moment forward.

Pretend that the business you own—or want to own—is the prototype, or will be the prototype, for 5,000 more just like it. That your business is going to serve as the model for 5,000 more just like it. Not *almost* like it, but *just* like it. Perfect replicates. Clones. In other words, pretend that you are going to franchise your business. (Note, I said *pretend*. I'm not saying that you *should*. That isn't necessary—unless, of course, you want to.)

Further, pretend that there are standards you have to abide by in order to pull this off. In other words, there are rules of the game.

These rules are:

1. The model will be operated by people with the lowest possible level of skill.
2. The model will stand out as a place of impeccable order.
3. All work in the model will be documented in Operations Manuals.
4. The model will provide a uniformly predictable service to the consumer.
5. The model will utilize a uniform color, dress, and facilities code.

Let's take a look at each of these rules in turn.

1. The Model Will Be Operated by People with the Lowest Possible Level of Skill

Yes, I said *lowest* possible level of skill. If your Model depends on highly skilled people, it's going to be impossible to replicate. Such people are at a premium in the marketplace. They're also expensive, thus raising the price you will have to charge for your product or service. The question you need to keep asking is: "How can I give my customer the results he wants *systematically,* rather than *personally?*" Put another way, "How can I create a business whose results are *systems*-dependent rather than *people-*dependent?"

That is not to say that people are unimportant. Quite the contrary. People bring systems to life. People make it possible for things that are *designed* to work to produce the intended results. And, in the process, they learn how to more effectively make things work for themselves and for your business.

It's been said, and I believe it to be true, that great businesses are not built by extraordinary people but by ordinary people doing extraordinary things. But for ordinary people to do extraordinary things a system—a "way of doing things"—is needed to compensate for the disparity between the skills your people have and the skills needed to produce the result.

In this context, the system becomes a tool your people use to increase their productivity to get the job done. It's *your* job to develop that tool and to teach your people how to use it. It's *their* job to use the tool you've developed and to recommend improvements based on their experience with it.

There's another reason for this rule—you might call it the Rule Of Ordinary People—that states that the blessing of ordinary people is that they make your job more *difficult.*

The typical owner of a small business prefers highly skilled people because he believes they make his job *easier* —he can simply leave the work to them. That is, Management by Abdication rather than by Delegation. The inevitable result is a business that depends totally on the whims and moods of its people. If they're in the mood, the job gets done. If they're not, it doesn't. "How do I motivate my people?" becomes the constant question. "How do I keep them in the mood?"

It is literally *impossible* to produce a consistent result in a business that is created around the need for extraordinary people. On the other hand, if you intentionally build your business on the skills of *ordinary* people, you will be forced to ask the difficult questions about how to produce a result *without* the extraordinary ones.

You will be forced to find a system that leverages your ordinary people to the point where they can produce extraordinary results. To find innovative system solutions to the people problems that have plagued business owners since the beginning of time. *To build a business that works.* You will be forced to do the work of business development, not as a replacement for people development but as its necessary correlate.

2. The Model Will Stand Out as a Place of Impeccable Order

At the core of Rule #2 is the irrepressible fact that in a world of chaos, most people crave order. And it doesn't take a genius to see that the world today is in a state of massive chaos. Wars, famine, violence, inflation, recession, a shifting of traditional forms of social interaction, the threat of nuclear holocaust—all are communicated instantly and continuously to the fixated consumer.

As Alvin Toffler writes in his revolutionary book, *The Third Wave,* ". . . most people surveying the world around them today see only chaos. They suffer a sense of personal powerlessness and pointlessness." He goes on to say that

"Individuals need life structure. A life lacking in comprehensive structure is an aimless wreck. The absence of structure breeds breakdown. Structure provides the relatively fixed points of reference we need."[1]

It is these "relatively fixed points of reference" that an orderly business provides its customer and its employees in an otherwise disorderly world. A business that looks orderly says to your customer that your people know what they're doing. A business that looks orderly says to your people that *you* know what you're doing. A business that looks orderly says that while the world may not work, some things can. A business that looks orderly says to your customer that he can trust in the result delivered, and assures your people that they can trust in their future with you.

A business that looks orderly says that the structure is in place.

3. All Work in the Model Will Be Documented in Operations Manuals

Documentation says, "This is how we do it here." Without it, all routinized work turns into exceptions. Documentation provides your people with the structure they need, and with a written account of how to "get the job done" in the most efficient and effective way. It communicates to the new employee, as well as to the old, that there is a logic to the world in which they have chosen to work, that there is a technology by which results are produced. Documentation is an affirmation of order.

Again from Toffler: ". . . . for many people, a job is crucial psychologically, over and above the paycheck. By

---

1. Alvin Toffler, *The Third Wave* (New York: William Morrow and Company, Inc. 1980), pp. 390, 389.

making clear demands on their time and energy, it provides an element of structure around which the rest of their lives can be organized."[2]

The operative word here is "clear." Documentation provides the clarity structure needs if it is to be meaningful to your people. Through documentation, structure is reduced to specific means rather than generalized ends, to a literal and simplified task The Technician in each of us needs to understand to do the job at hand.

The Operations Manual—the repository of the documentation—is therefore best described as a company's How-To-Do-It Guide. It designates the purpose of the work, specifies the steps needed to be taken while doing that work, and summarizes the standards associated with both the process and the result.

Your Prototype would not be a Model without one.

4. The Model Will Provide a Uniformly Predictable Service to the Consumer

While the business must look orderly, it is not sufficient; the business must also *act* orderly. It must do things in a predictable, uniform way.

An experience I had not too long ago illustrates the point.

I went to a barber who, in our first meeting, gave me one of the best haircuts I had ever had. He was a master with the scissors and used them exlusively, never resorting to electric shears as so many others do. Before cutting my hair, he insisted on washing it, explaining that the washing made cutting easier. During the haircut, one of his assistants kept my cup of coffee fresh. In all, the experience was delightful, so I made an appointment to return.

2. Alvin Toffler, *The Third Wave*, p. 389.

When I returned, however, everything had changed. Instead of using the scissors exclusively, he used the shears about 50 percent of the time. He not only didn't wash my hair, but never even mentioned it. The assistant *did* bring me a cup of coffee, but only once, never to return. Nonetheless, the haircut was again excellent.

Several weeks later, I returned for a third appointment. This time, the barber did wash my hair, but *after* cutting it, preliminary to a final trim. This time he again used the scissors exclusively, but, unlike the first two times, no coffee was served, although he did ask if I would like a glass of wine. At first I thought it might be the assistant's day off, but she soon appeared, busily working with the inventory near the front of the shop.

As I left, something in me decided not to go back. It certainly wasn't the haircut—he did an excellent job. It wasn't the barber. He was pleasant, affable, seemed to know his business. It was something more essential than that.

There was absolutely no consistency to the experience.

The expectations created at the first meeting were violated at each subsequent visit. I wasn't sure what to expect. And something in me *wanted* to be sure. I wanted an experience *I* could repeat by making the choice to return.

The unpredictability said nothing about the barber, other than that he was constantly—and *arbitrarily*—changing my experience for me. *He* was in control of my experience, not I. And he demonstrated little sensitivity to the impact of his behavior on me. He was running the business for *him*, not for me. And by doing so, he was depriving me of the experience of making a decision to patronize his business for my own reasons, whatever they might have been.

It didn't matter what I wanted. It didn't matter that I enjoyed the sound of the scissors and somehow equated them with a professional haircut. It didn't matter that I enjoyed being waited on by his assistant. It didn't matter that I enjoyed the experience of having my hair washed before he set to work and that I actually believed it would improve the quality of the haircut. I would have been embarrassed to *ask* for these things, let alone to give my reasons for wanting them. They were all so totally emotional, so illogical. How could I have explained them, or justified them, without appearing to be a boob?

What the barber did was to give me a delightful experience, and *then take it away.*

It reminded me of my first psychology course in college. I recall the professor talking about the "Burnt Child" Syndrome. This is where a child is alternately punished and rewarded for the same kind of behavior. This form of behavior in a parent can be disastrous to the child; he never knows what to expect or how to act. It can also be disastrous to the customer. The "Burnt Child," of course, has no choice but to stay with the parent. But the "Burnt Customer" can go someplace else. And he will.

What you do in your Model is not nearly as important as doing what you do the same way, each and every time.

5. The Model Will Utilize a Uniform Color, Dress, and Facilities Code

Marketing studies tell us that all consumers are moved to act by the colors and shapes they find in the marketplace. Different consumer groups simply respond differently to specific colors and shapes.

Believe it or not, the colors and shapes of your Model can make or break your business!

65

Louis Cheskin, founder of The Color Research Institute in California, wrote about the power of colors and shapes in his book, *Why People Buy.*

Little things that are meaningless from a practical point of view may have great emotional meaning through their symbolism. Images and colors are often great motivating forces.

Some time ago we conducted a study of women shopping in an apparel shop. A young woman wanted to buy a blouse that was available in several colors. She held the blue blouse up to her face and looked into the mirror. She was a blonde and she knew she looked good in blue. She fingered the red one lovingly. She loved the color, she thought, but she said it was too strong and loud. The salesgirl reminded her that yellow was the fashionable color. She could not make up her mind between the color that she looked best in, the color she liked best and the color in current fashion, so she settled on a grey blouse. It was reported to me a couple of weeks later that she didn't like the grey blouse. 'It was dead,' she said. She wore it only twice.

Some of the other purchasers of blouses permitted one of the inner drives to win. Some bought blouses because the color flattered them; others chose the color that was in fashion and some took the color they liked. Each chose a color that satisfied the strongest urge or fulfilled the greatest wish. Just think! All this deep psychology in the mere process of buying a blouse.[3]

3. Louis Cheskin, *Why People Buy* (New York: Liveright Publishing Corporation, 1959), p. 119.

Your business is the same as the blouse in Cheskin's story. There are colors that work and colors that don't. The colors you show your consumer must be scientifically determined and then used throughout your Model—on the walls, the floors, the ceiling, the vehicles, the invoices, your people's clothes, the displays, the signage. The Model must be thought of as a package for your one and only product—your business.

Just as with colors, there are shapes that work and shapes that don't, on your business card, your signage, your logo, your merchandise displays. In one test, Cheskin showed that a triangle produced far fewer sales than a circle, and a crest outproduced both by a significant margin! Imagine, sales increased or lost by the choice of a seemingly meaningless shape!

The shape of your sign, your logo, the typestyle used on your business cards not only can have a significant impact on sales, but will, whether you care to think about it or not!

Your Prototype must be packaged as carefuly as any box of cereal.

■ ■

Before we go on, let's summarize what we've covered so far.

Go to work *on* your business rather than *in* it.

Go to work on your business as if it were the preproduction prototype of a mass-produceable product.

Think of your business as something apart from yourself, as a world of its own, as a product of your efforts, as a machine designed to fulfill a very specific need, as a mechanism for giving you more life, as a system of interconnecting parts, as a package of cereal, as a can of beans, as something created to satisfy your consumers' deeply held

67

perceived needs, as a place that acts distinctly different from all other places, as a solution to somebody else's problem.

Think of your business as anything but a job!

Go to work *on* your business rather than *in* it, and ask yourself the following questions:

- "How can I get my business to work, but without me?"
- "How can I get my people to work, but without my constant interference?"
- "How can I systematize my business in such a way that it could be replicated 5,000 times, so the 5000th unit would run as smoothly as the first?"
- "How can I own the business, and still be free of it?"
- "How can I spend my time doing the work I love to do rather than the work I *have* to do?"

If you ask yourself these questions, you'll eventually come face-to-face with the *real* problem: *that you don't know the answers!*

And that's been the problem all along!

But now it should be different. *Because now you know that you don't know.* Now you are ready to look the problem squarely in the face.

The problem isn't your business. The problem is *you.* It's always been you and will always be you until you change. Until you change your perspective about what a business is and how it works. Until you begin to think about your business in a totally new way.

Business is both an art and a science. And, like art and science, serious business calls for specific information. Most importantly, serious business calls for a process, a practice, by which to obtain that information, and then a method to use that information productively.

What follows is just such a method. A programmed approach to learning what needs to be learned in order to climb the proverbial ladder. A proven way to the top that has been successfully implemented by thousands of businesses.

We call it The Michael Thomas Business Development Program.

PART III

Building a Business That Works!

10

THE BUSINESS DEVELOPMENT PROCESS

"Tolerance for failure is a very specific part of the excellent company culture—and that lesson comes directly from the top. Champions have to make lots of tries and consequently suffer some failures or the organization won't learn."

Thomas J. Peters and Robert H. Waterman Jr.
In Search of Excellence

B uilding the Prototype of your business is a continuous process—a Business Development Process. Its foundation is three distinct, yet thoroughly integrated activities through which your business can pursue its natural evolution. They are: Innovation, Quantification, and Orchestration.

Innovation

Innovation is often thought of as creativity. But as Harvard Professor Theodore Levitt points out, the difference between creativity and innovation is the difference between *thinking* about getting things done in the world and *getting* things done. Says Professor Levitt, "Creativity thinks up new things. Innovation does new things."[1]

The Franchise Revolution has brought with it an application of innovation that has been almost universally ignored by American business. By recognizing that it is not the *commodity* that demands innovation but the *process* by which it is sold, the franchisor aims his innovative energies at the way in which his business does business.

To the franchisor, the entire process by which the business does business is a marketing tool, a mechanism for finding and keeping customers. Each and every component of the business system is a means through which the franchisor can differentiate his business from all other businesses in the mind of his consumer.

Where the *business* is the product, how the business interacts with the consumer is more important than what it sells.

Innovation doesn't have to be expensive to be effective. Some of the most powerful innovations have required little more than the change of a few words, a gesture, the color of clothing.

For example, what does the salesperson in a retail store invariably say to the incoming customer? He says, "May I help you?" And what does the customer invariably respond? He says, "No thanks, just looking." Have you heard that one before?

Now why do you suppose the salesperson asks that question when he *knows* that the customer will respond the way he does? Because the customer responds the way he does, that's why! If the customer is just looking, the salesperson won't have to go to work!

Can you imagine what those few words are costing

---

1. Theodore Levitt, *Marketing for Business Growth*, p. 71.

retailers in this country in lost sales? Here's a perfect opportunity to try a simple and inexpensive innovation.

THE INNOVATION   Instead of asking, "May I help you?" try "Hi, have you been in here before?" The customer will respond with either a yes or no. In either case, you are then free to pursue the conversation.

If the answer is yes, you can say, "Great. We've created a special new program for people who've shopped here before. Let me take just a minute to tell you about it."

If the answer is no, you can say, "Great, we've created a special new program for people who *haven't* shopped here before. Let me take just a minute to tell you about it."

Of course, you'll have to have created a special new program to talk about in either case. But, that's the easy part.

Just think. A few simple words. Nothing fancy. But, the result will put money in your pocket. How much? That depends. But, in judging by the experience of our clients, sales will increase between 10 and 16 percent almost immediately!

Think about it: a few words. And sales instantly go up.

THE INNOVATION   Again, for salespeople, a six-week test. For the first three weeks wear a brown suit to work, a starched tan shirt, a brown tie (for men) and well-polished brown shoes. Make certain that all the elements of your suit are clean and well-pressed. For the following three weeks wear a navy blue suit (three-piece for men, two-piece for women), a good, starched white shirt, a tie with red in it (a pin, a scarf, or a necklace with red in it for women), and highly polished black shoes.

The result will be dramatic: Sales will go up during the second three-week period! Why? Because, as our clients have consistently discovered, blue suits outsell brown suits! *And it doesn't matter who's in them.*

THE INNOVATION   The next time you want somebody to do something for you, touch him softly on the arm as you ask him to do it. You will be amazed to find that more people will respond positively when you touch them than when you don't.

Again, to apply this to your business, you or your salespeople should make a point of touching each customer on the elbow, arm, or back some time during the sales process. You will find, as our clients have found, that there will be a measurable increase in sales.

Innovation is the heart of every successful business. It asks the question: "What is standing in the way of my customer getting what he wants from my business?" It *always* takes the customer's point of view. At the same time, innovation simplifies your business to its critical essentials. It should make things easier in your business; otherwise it's not innovation but complication.

Innovation is the mechanism through which your business identifies itself in the mind of your consumer and establishes its individuality. It is the result of a scientifically generated and quantifiably verified profile of your consumer's perceived needs.

Innovation is the signature of a bold, imaginative hand.

Quantification

But innovation by itself leads nowhere. It needs to be quantified. Without quantification, how would you know whether the innovation worked?

By quantification, I'm talking about the numbers related to your marketing process that are recorded and used to find and keep customers.

Ask any group of small business owners how many selling opportunities they had the day before (as we have at The Michael Thomas Corporation time after time) and *99 percent of them won't know the answer.* Quantification is not done in most businesses. And it's costing them a fortune!

For example, how would you know that changing the words you use to greet an incoming customer produced a 16 percent increase in sales unless you quantified the impact of those words by, 1) counting the number of selling opportunities you had; 2) counting the number of people who purchased; and, 3) determining the unit value of the sale? These numbers enable you to determine the precise value of your innovation.

How would you know that wearing a blue suit had a specific monetary impact on your business unless you quantified that impact? The answer is obvious; you wouldn't.

Few companies *do* quantify such things, even those that believe in quantification. Because few believe that such apparently insignificant innovations are really that important!

But ask yourself, if you could increase sales 10 percent by doing something as simple a wearing a blue suit, would you do it? Would you *make* it important? The answer is as obvious as the question is ridiculous. Of course you would!

And it is the obvious that must be addressed by quantification at the outset of the Business Development Process.

Begin by quantifying everything related to how you do

business. I mean *everything*. How many customers do you see in person each day? How many in the morning? In the afternoon? How many people call your business each day? How many call to ask for a price? How many want to purchase something? How many of product X are sold each day? How many each week? Which days are busiest? How busy? And so forth.

You can't ask too many questions about the numbers. Eventually, you and your people will think of your entire business in terms of the numbers. You'll quantify everything. You'll be able to read your business's health chart by the flow of the numbers. You'll know which numbers are critical and which are not. You'll become as familiar with your business's numbers as your doctor is with your blood pressure and pulse rates.

Without the numbers you can't possibly know where you are, let alone where you're going. With the numbers, your business will take on a totally new meaning.

It will come alive with possibilities.

Orchestration

Once you innovate a process and quantify its impact on your business, once you find something that works better than what preceded it, once you discover how to increase the "yeses" from your customers—at that point, it's time to orchestrate the whole thing.

Orchestration is the elimination of discretion, or choice, from the operating level of your business. Without it, nothing could be planned, and nothing anticipated—by you or your customer. For as Theodore Levitt says, "Discretion is the enemy of order, standardization, and quality."[2]

"If a blue suit works, wear it every single time you're in front of a customer," is the dictum from the disciples of Orchestration.

Every great Business Format Franchise company knows one thing to be true: If you haven't orchestrated it, you don't own it. And if you don't own it, you can't depend on it. And if you can't depend on it, you haven't got a franchise.

Orchestration is based on the absolutely quantifiable certainty that people will do only one thing predictably—*be unpredictable.*

For your business to be predictable, your people must be. But if people aren't predictable, then what? The system must provide the predictability. To do what? To give your customer what he wants every single time. Why? Because unless your customer gets everything he wants every single time he'll go someplace else to get it!

Orchestration is the glue that holds you fast to your customer's perceptions. It is the certainty which is absent from every other human experience. It is the order and the logic behind man's craving for reason. It is as simple as doing what you do, saying what you say, looking like you look—being how you are—for as long as that works.

And when it doesn't work any longer, change it. The Business Development Process is not static. It's not something you do and then are done with. *It's something you do all the time.*

Once you've innovated, quantified and orchestrated

---

2. Theodore Levitt, *Marketing for Business Growth* (New York: McGraw-Hill, 1974), p. 56.

something in your business, you must *continue* to innovate, quantify, and orchestrate it. Because the world, moving as it does, will not tolerate a stationary object. It will
collide with what you've created, and sooner or later destroy it.

Innovation, Quantification, and Orchestration are the
backbone of every extraordinary business. They are the es-
sence of your Business Development Program.

11
YOUR BUSINESS
DEVELOPMENT PROGRAM

"And I say to ye all, good friends, that as ye grow in golf, ye come to see the things ye learn there in every other place. The grace that comes from such a discipline, the extra feel in the hands, the extra strength and knowin', all those special powers ye've felt from time to time, begin to enter our lives."

Michael Murphy
Golf in the Kingdom

Now you understand the task ahead: to think of your business as though it were the prototype for 5,000 more just like it. To imagine that someone will walk through your door with the intention of buying your business—but only if it works. And only if it works without a lot of work and without *you* to work it.

Imagine yourself at that moment. Imagine your smile inside as you say, "Let me show you how it works," knowing that not only will it work, but it will work better than any business he's ever seen.

Imagine yourself taking the potential buyer through your business, explaining each component and how it works with every other component. How you've innovated systems solutions to people problems, how you've quantified the results of those innovations, and how you've orchestrated the innovations so that they produce the same results every single time.

Imagine yourself introducing the potential buyer of your business to your people, and standing by while they proudly explain their accountabilities to the fascinated stranger.

Imagine how impressed the potential buyer of your business would be upon being presented with such order, such predictability, such irreproachable control.

Imagine the results of your Business Development Program.

Your Business Development Program is the step-by-step process through which you convert your existing business (or the one you're about to create) into a perfectly organized Model for thousands more just like it. Your Business Development Program is the process through which you create your Franchise Prototype.

The process we have developed is composed of seven distinct steps:

- Your Primary Aim
- Your Strategic Objective
- Your Organizational Strategy
- Your Management Strategy
- Your People Strategy
- Your Marketing Strategy
- Your Systems Strategy.

Let's get started.

12

YOUR PRIMARY AIM

"The chief characteristics of the volitional act is the existence of a *purpose* to be achieved; the clear vision of an aim."

Robert Assagioli
The Act of Will

Y ou'll be surprised to find out that your business is not the first order of business on our agenda. *You are.*

Your business is not your life, though it plays a significantly important role in your life. Before you can determine what that role will be, you must ask yourself. "What do I value most? What kind of lifestyle do I want? What do I want my life to look like, to feel like?"

Your Primary Aim is the answer to those questions.

Consider it from another perspective.

I'd like you to imagine that you are about to attend one of the most important occasions of your life. It will be held in a room sufficiently large to seat all of your friends, family, and business associates—anyone and everyone to whom you are important and who is important to you.

The walls are draped with lovely muted tapestries.

The lighting is subdued, soft, casting a warm glow on the faces of your expectant guests. Their chairs are handsomely upholstered in a fabric that matches the tapestries. The carpeting is deeply piled. At the front of the room is a dais, and on the dais a large, beautifully decorated table, with candles burning at either end.

On the table, in the center, is the object of everyone's attention. A large, shining, ornate box. And in the box is ... you! Stiff as a proverbial board.

Do you see yourself lying in the box, not a dry eye in the room? Now, listen. From the four corners of the room comes a tape recording of your voice. You're addressing your guests. You're telling them the story of your life.

How would you like that story to go?

That's your Primary Aim.

What would you like to able to say about your life after it's too late to do anything about it?

That's your Primary Aim.

If you were to write a script for the tape to be played for the mourners at your funeral, how would you like it to read?

That's your Primary Aim.

And once you've created the script, *all you need to do is make it come true.* All you need to do is begin living your life as if it were important. All you need to do is take your life seriously. To create it intentionally. To actively make your life into the life you wish it to be.

Simple? Yes. Easy? No. But absolutely essential if your business is to have any meaning beyond work. Because your business is going to become an integral part of that tape, a major contributor to the realization of your dream, a significant component of your Primary Aim.

Do you see why your Primary Aim is so important to the success of your business? With no clear picture of how you want your life to be, how on earth could you begin to live it?

How would you know what first step to take? How would you measure your progress? How would you know where you were? How would you know how far you had gone? How would you know how much farther you had yet to go?

Without your Primary Aim, you wouldn't. Indeed, you *couldn't*. It would be virtually impossible.

As with Mature companies, great people are those who know how they got where they are and how to get where they're going. Great people have a vision of their lives which they practice emulating each and every day. Their lives are spent living out the vision they have of their future in the present. And each and every day they compare what they've done with what they intended to do. And where there's a disparity between the two, they don't wait very long to make up the difference.

I believe it's true that the difference between great people and everyone else is that great people create their lives actively, while everyone else is created *by* their lives, passively waiting to see where life takes them next.

The difference between the two is the difference between living fully and just existing.

So before you start your business, or before you return to it tomorrow, ask yourself the following questions:

- "What do I want my life to look like?"
- "How do I want my life to feel on a day-to-day basis?"
- "What would I like to be able to say I truly know in my life, about my life?"
- "How would I like to be with other people in my life—my family, my friends, my business associates, my customers, my community?"

- "How would I like people to think about me?"
- "What would I like to be doing two years from now? Ten years from now? Twenty years from now?"
- "What specifically would I like to learn during my life—spiritually, physically, financially, technically, intellectually? About relationships?"
- "How much money will I need to do the things I want to do? By when will I need it?"

These are just a few of the questions you might ask yourself in the creation of your Primary Aim. The answers to them become the standards against which you can begin to measure your life's progress. In the absence of such standards your life will drift aimlessly, without purpose, without meaning.

Your Primary Aim is the vision necessary to bring your business to life and your life to your business.

It provides you with a purpose.

It provides you with energy.

It provides you with the grist for your day-to-day mill.

13

YOUR STRATEGIC OBJECTIVE

" 'Your arrows do not carry,' observed the Master, 'because they do not reach far enough spiritually.' "

Eugen Herrigel
Zen in the Art of Archery

Once you have a picture of how you want your life to be, you can turn to the business that's going to help you realize it. You can turn to the development of your Strategic Objective.

Your Strategic Objective is a *very clear* statement of what your business has to ultimately do to make your Primary Aim possible. It is the vision of the finished product that is and will be your business. In this context, your business is a means rather than an end, a vehicle to enrich your life rather than a vehicle that wastes what life you have.

Your Strategic Objective is *not* a business plan. Business plans are marketing tools, not business development tools. They're created to convince someone else that you have a worthwhile business, not to help you build one. Not that you shouldn't have a business plan. You should.

But unless your plan can be reduced to a set of simple and clearly stated standards, it will do more to confuse you than to help.

Your Strategic Objective is just such a list of standards. It is a tool for measuring your progress toward a specific end. It is designed for implementation, not for rationalization. It is a template for your business, to make certain that the time you invest in it produces exactly what you want from it.

Let's take a closer look at some of the standards that need to be included in your Strategic Objective.

The First Standard: Money

The first standard of your Strategic Objective is money. Gross revenues. How big is your vision? How big will your company be when it's finally done? Will it be a three hundred thousand dollar company? A one million dollar company? A five hundred million dollar company? If you don't know the answer, how can you possibly know whether you will realize your Primary Aim?

But gross revenues alone are not enough. You also have to know what your gross profits are going to be, your net pre-tax profits, your net after-tax profits. At this point you come face-to-face with the first dilemma encountered by everyone going into business. How can you possibly know now what your business is going to produce in sales that far in the future?

The answer is, you can't! But it doesn't matter. At the beginning of your business, *any* standards are better than *no* standards. Creating money standards is not just strategically necessary for your *business*, it is strategically necessary for your *life*, for the realization of your Primary

Aim. Indeed, the first question you must always ask when creating standards for your Strategic Objective is: "What will serve my Primary Aim?"

The first question about money then becomes, "How much money do I need to live the way I wish?" Not in income, but in assets. In other words, how much money do you need in order to be *independent* of work, to be free?

Remember—first your life, then your business.

Once you have that number, you can then ask the second question in the creation of standards for your Strategic Objective: "What kind of business will provide me with the amount of money I'll need to be independent of work?"

At this point another set of standards are immediately brought into the picture. Because once you've created a set of financial standards for your life, it becomes obvious that the business must have a realistic chance of achieving them. How do you know whether or not it does? By engaging in an orderly process of "assumption and discovery." First *assume* certain things to be true, and then *discover* whether or not they are.

And the first assumption you have to make is that your business is an Opportunity Worth Pursuing.

The Second Standard: An Opportunity Worth Pursuing

An Opportunity Worth Pursuing is a business that can fulfill the financial standards you created for your Primary Aim and your Strategic Objective.

If it is reasonable to assume that it can, the business is worth pursuing. If it is unreasonable to assume that it can, then no matter how exciting, interesting, or appealing the business is, forget it. Walk away from it. It will consume too much of your precious time and prevent you from finding a true Opportunity Worth Pursuing.

How do you know whether you have an Opportunity Worth Pursuing? Look around. Ask yourself, "Does the business I have in mind alleviate a frustration experienced by a large enough group of consumers to make it worth my while?"

This standard fulfills two primary requirements of your Strategic Objective. It tells you what *kind* of business you're creating and, at the same time, defines who your *customer* will be. It tells you what you need to sell and to whom.

What Kind of Business Am I in?

Ask anyone what kind of business they're in, and they'll instinctively respond with the name of the commodity they sell. "We're in the computer business." Or, "We're in the hot tub business." Always the commodity, never the product.

What's the difference? The commodity is the thing your customer actually walks out with in his hand. The product is what your customer *feels* as he walks out of your business. What he feels about your business, *not* the commodity. Understanding the difference between the two is what a successful business is all about.

Charles Revson, the founder of Revlon and an extraordinarily successful entrepreneur, once said about his company: "In the factory Revlon manufactures cosmetics, but in the store Revlon sells hope."

The commodity is cosmetics; the product, hope.

In a 1984 Chanel television commercial, an incredibly handsome man and a strikingly beautiful woman are alone while music plays hypnotically in the background. The scene shifts quickly and frequently to other shots, such as a tall, erect building. So far there hasn't been a sound except for the music that supports this suggestive visual ballet. The black shadow of an airplane moves vertically up the building. She approaches him. The music continues. He says, "Can I ask you a question?" in a voice filled with intimacy and invitation. We don't hear her answer. We just see her tilt her head back, close her eyes, and open her mouth slightly.

Suddenly, the message: "Share the Fantasy. Chanel."

Not a word about perfume. That's the commodity. The commercial is selling the product—fantasy. The commercial is saying, "Buy Chanel and this fantasy can be yours."

What's *your* product? What feeling will your customer walk away with? Peace of mind? Order? Power? Love? What is he *really* buying when he buys from you?

The truth is, nobody's interested in the commodity. People buy feelings. And as the world becomes more and more complex, and the commodities more varied, the feelings we want become more urgent, less rational, more unconscious. How your business anticipates those feelings *and satisfies them* is your product. And the demographics and psychographics associated with your customer will predetermine how you do that.

Who Is My Customer?

Every business has what is called a Central Demographic Model. That is, a most probable consumer. And that consumer has a whole set of characteristics through which you can define him—age, sex, income, family status, education, profession, and so forth.

Demographics is the science of marketplace reality. It tells you *who* your customer is.

Your Central Demographic Model consumer buys for very particular reasons, none of which are rational or even explicable! Yet he buys, or doesn't. The motivations that propel him in either direction constitute your Central Psychographic Model.

Psychographics is the science of *perceived* marketplace reality. It tells you *why* your customer buys.

So when you ask, "Is this business an Opportunity Worth Pursuing?" the only way to tell is to determine how many selling opportunities you will have (your customer's demographics) and how successfully you can satisfy the emotional or perceived needs lurking there (your customer's psychographics).

Standards Three Through?

There is no specific number of standards in your Strategic Objective. There are only specific questions that need to be answered.

- *When* is your Prototype going to be completed? In two years? Three? Ten?
- *Where* are you going to be in business? Locally? Regionally? Nationally? Internationally?
- *How* are you going to be in business? Retail? Wholesale? A combination of the two?
- What standards are you going to insist upon regarding reporting, cleanliness, clothing, management, hiring, firing, training, and so forth?

You can begin to see that the standards you create for your business will shape both your business and the experience you have of your business. In fact, the standards of your Strategic Objective create the tension that draws the future model of your business and the way it actually appears today closer to one another.

As we saw earlier, standards create the energy by which the best companies, and the most effective people, produce results.

14

YOUR ORGANIZATIONAL STRATEGY

> "All organizations are hierarchical. At each level people serve under those above them. An organization is therefore a structured institution. If it is not structured, it is a mob. Mobs do not get things done, they destroy things."
>
> *Theodore Levitt*
> *Marketing for Business Growth*

E veryone wants to "get organized." But when you suggest that they can start by creating an Organization Chart, all you get is doubtful—and sometimes hostile—stares.

"Don't be ridiculous," a client once retorted. "We're just a small company. We don't need an Organization Chart. We need better people!"

Despite his protestations, I persisted. Because I knew something he didn't. I knew that the organizational development reflected in the Organization Chart can have a more profound impact on a company than any other single business development step.

Organizing Around Personalities

Most companies organize around personalities rather than functions. That is, around people rather than accountabilities.

The result is almost always chaos.

To best show you what I mean, let's take a look at Widget Makers, a new company formed by Jack and Murray Hopeful, brothers and now partners, in an enterprise that they are *sure* will make them rich.

Jack and Murray start their partnership as most do, by sharing the work. When Jack's not making the widget, Murray is. When Jack's not helping the customer, Murray is. When Murray's not doing the books, Jack is. The business hums like a well-oiled machine. The shop is spotless. The windows gleam. The floors are meticulous. The customers smile. And Jack and Murray bustle.

Taking turns, always taking turns.

On Monday, Murray opens up. On Tuesday, Jack. On Wednesday, Murray. On Thursday, Jack. After all, they're partners aren't they? If *they* don't do it, who *will?* It's only fair that they share the work.

They go on that way, and the business begins to grow.

All of a sudden, there's more work than either Murray or Jack can handle. They have to get help. So they hire Jerry. A great guy. And a nephew to boot. As long as they have to pay someone, might as well keep it in the family.

Now it's Jack, Murray and Jerry, taking turns, taking turns. When Jack's not doing the books, Murray is. And when Murray and Jack aren't, Jerry is. Now when Murray isn't working with a customer, either Jack or Jerry is. Or when Jack isn't opening up, Murray is, or Jerry. Things are moving. The business is jumping. Jack and Murray and Jerry are as busy as three people can be.

Herb joins them. Jack's wife's brother. A good guy. A hard worker. Willing and eager.

Now it's Jack, Murray, Jerry, and Herb, taking turns, taking turns. When Jack's not doing the books, Herb is, or Murray, or Jerry. When Murray's not working with a customer, it's Jack or Jerry or Herb. When Jerry's not making widgets, it's Murray or Jack or Herb. Everybody's opening up, answering the telephone, going out for sandwiches, making deposits—taking turns, taking turns, taking turns.

But soon the widgets begin to come back. They don't seem to be working. "We never had this trouble before." says Jack to Murray. Murray looks at Herb. Herb looks at Jerry.

All of a sudden, the books begin to look funny. "We never had this trouble before," says Murray to Jack. Jack looks at Jerry. Jerry looks at Herb.

And that's not all. The shop is beginning to fall apart. Tools are missing. Dust is getting in the widgets. Corrugated cardboard is strewn about the work table. Nails are in the screw boxes and screws in the nail boxes. Jack and Murray and Jerry and Herb are beginning to bump into each other on their way in, on their way out. They're elbowing for room in the work space.

Windows aren't getting cleaned. Floors aren't getting swept. Tempers begin to mount. But who's to say something? And what? And to whom? If everybody's doing everything, then who's accountable for anything?

If Jack and Murray are partners, who's in charge? If both, then what happens when Jack tells Jerry to do something that Murray won't allow him to do? When Herb wants to go for lunch, who does he tell—Jack? Murray? Jerry? Who's accountable for making certain that the store is manned?

When the widgets go bad, who's accountable for correcting the condition? When the books are unbalanced, who's accountable for balancing them? When the floors need cleaning, when the windows need washing, when the shop needs opening or closing, when the customers need tending—who's accountable for producing the results?

Without an Organization Chart, everything hinges

upon luck and good feelings, upon the personalities of the people and the good will they share. Unfortunately, personalities, good feelings, good will, and luck aren't the ingredients of successful organization but the recipe instead for chaos and disaster.

Organization needs something more.

Organizing Your Company

Let's start Widget Makers all over again.

Jack and Murray Hopeful are sitting in their kitchen. They have decided to form Widget Makers. They are excited about its prospects but know that if it's to succeed they have to approach it differently from the way most people start a new business.

The first thing they decide to do is to incorporate. Having both worked in partnerships with other people—and failed—Jack and Murray know that there's nothing more disastrous than a partnership. Unless it's a family business, that is. Family businesses are even *worse* than partnerships. But a partnership that's *also* a family business? No. Jack and Murray decide to do it a different way.

Sitting there at the kitchen table, Jack and Murray each take a blank piece of paper and print their names at the top of the page. Under each name they print "Primary Aim." For the next hour or so, Jack and Murray each visualize how he would like his life to look and writes his conclusions on the page in front of him.

Then they spend another hour or so talking about what they wrote, sharing their personal dreams with each other, perhaps discovering in that hour more about each other than they had known in all their years as brothers.

The next step Jack and Murray take is to pick the

97

Chief Executive Officer or Chairman of the Board of their new corporation. They ponder the question seriously. This is the person who will ultimately be accountable to Jack and Murray for the realization of their dream.

Murray decides that Jack should do it. Although Murray is the older brother, Jack has always taken his accountabilities more seriously. Their life savings are at stake here. If the business is to give them both what they want, someone will have to take it very seriously indeed.

They decide on Jack for CEO.

The next step will require some time: the creation of the Strategic Objective for Widget Makers, Inc. Jack, as CEO, assigns Murray, as a member of the Board, the accountability to do the necessary research concerning the Central Demographic Model they have tentatively chosen. How many potential buyers are there in the territory in which they've decided to do business? Is the population growing? What is the competition? How are widgets priced and how are they selling? Is there a future for widgets in the territory? What is the anticipated growth of the territory? Any zoning changes expected?

Jack also asks Murray to create a questionnaire and mail it to a sample of their Central Demographic Model consumers to find out how they feel they're treated by other widget companies. At the same time, Murray is to personally call 150 of those consumers. He'll conduct a Needs Analysis to get a better understanding of how they think and feel about widgets. What do widgets mean to them? How have widgets changed their lives? If they could have any kind of widget at all, what would it look like? How would it feel to use it? What do they want a good widget to do for them?

Murray agrees to do the research by a certain date.

Meanwhile, Jack will prepare the tentative financial materials needed to secure a loan from the bank—an operating pro forma and a cash flow projection for the first year of operation. Once the information about the consumer, the competition, and the pricing is collected, Jack and Murray will meet again and complete their Strategic Objective and plug in the final numbers needed for the loan.

Luck is with them. The information Murray collects about their Central Demographic Model, the competition, and the pricing is more than encouraging. They complete their Strategic Objective and then begin the task of Organizational Development—the creation of their Organization Chart.

Since their Strategic Objective has indicated *how* they will be doing business (one location, assembling and selling widgets and widget-related accessories to a specific consumer within the territory described as North Marine West), Jack and Murray determine that their Organization Chart will require the following positions:

- President and Chief Operating Officer (COO), accountable for the overall achievement of the Strategic Objective and reporting to the Chief Executive Officer (CEO);

- Vice President/Marketing, accountable for finding customers and finding new ways to provide customers with the satisfactions they derive from widgets, at lower cost, and with greater ease;

- Vice President/Operations, accountable for keeping customers by delivering to them what is promised by Marketing, and for discovering new ways of assembling widgets, at lower cost, and with greater efficiency so as to provide the customer with better service; and,

- Vice President/Finance, accountable for supporting both Marketing and Operations in the fulfillment of their accountabilities by maintaining a balanced financial posture in the community, and by securing capital whenever it's needed, and at the best rates.

- Reporting to the Vice President/Marketing are two positions: Sales Manager and Advertising/Research Manager.

- Reporting to the Vice President/Operations are three positions: Production Manager, Service Manager, and Facilities Manager.

- Reporting to the Vice President/Finance are two positions: Accounts Receivable Manager and Accounts Payable Manager.

Jack and Murray sit back and look at the Organization Chart of Widget Makers, Inc., and smile. It sure looks like a big company. The only problem is that *Jack and Murray's names will have to fill all the boxes! They're the only two employees.*

But what they have effectively done is describe all the work that's going to be done in Widget Makers, Inc. *when its full potential is realized.* More importantly, they have described the work that has to be done right away! Jack and Murray realize that there's no difference between the Widget Makers of today and the Widget Makers of tomorrow. The work is the same. Only the faces will change.

The next job Jack and Murray take on is writing a Position Contract for each position on their Organization Chart. A Position Contract (as we call it at The Michael

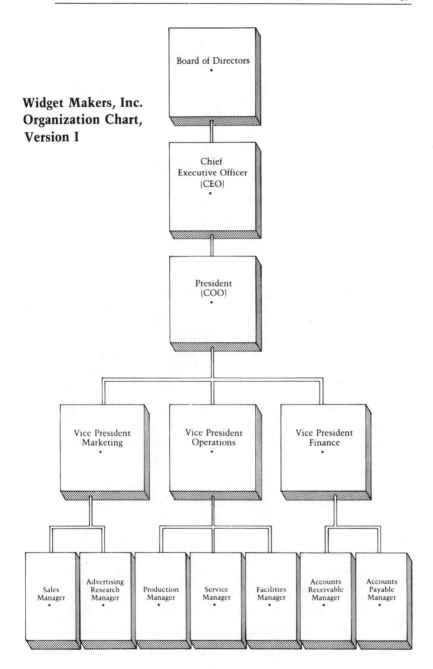

**Widget Makers, Inc.
Organization Chart,
Version I**

Board of Directors

Chief
Executive Officer
(CEO)

President
(COO)

Vice President
Marketing

Vice President
Operations

Vice President
Finance

Sales
Manager

Advertising
Research
Manager

Production
Manager

Service
Manager

Facilities
Manager

Accounts
Receivable
Manager

Accounts
Payable
Manager

101

Thomas Corporation) is a summary of the results to be achieved by each position in the company, the work the occupant of that position must do, a list of standards by which the results are to be evaluated, and a line for the signature of the person who agrees to fulfill those accountabilities.

A Position Contract is *not* a job description. It is a contract between the company and an employee, a summary of the rules of the game. It provides each person in an organization with a sense of commitment and accountability. Accountability literally means "stand up and be counted." The Position Contract is the document that identifies who's to stand up and what they're being counted on to produce.

Having completed the Position Contracts, Jack and Murray proceed to the most critical task of their new association: *naming the people to put in the boxes*. And since there are only two of them, it becomes even more critical if they're to avoid the errors of their past.

Since Jack is the Chief Executive Officer, Murray immediately votes to make him President. If he's going to be running the show, he'd better have the *authority* to run it. Jack accepts, and signs the Position Contract for the position of President, first as the CEO and then as the COO.

Now come the three Vice Presidential positions: Marketing, Operations, and Finance.

Jack asks Murray if he would agree to be Vice President/Marketing, since he did such an exceptional job on the marketing research project at the outset of their venture. Murray agrees, and signs the Vice President/Marketing Position Contract. Jack then signs Murray's Position Contract as the President (the Vice President/Marketing's manager) on behalf of the company.

Next comes Vice President/Operations. Jack agrees to take this position because it will be difficult for Murray to both sell the widgets and make them at the same time. This time he signs the Position Contract both as Vice President/Operations and as President.

Finally, Jack takes on the accountability of Vice President/Finance.

Murray now assumes the positions of Sales Manager and Advertising/Research Manager. Jack takes the positions of Production Manager, Service Manager, and Facilities Manager, as well as those of Accounts Payable Manager and Accounts Receivable Manager.

With all Position Contracts signed, Jack and Murray sit back for a second time to survey what they've done. When they see it, they're shocked! Jack has been given eight jobs, to Murray's three!

Something's got to be changed. After some thought, they agree to have Murray take on the accountabilities of Accounts Receivable and Accounts Payable, as well as that of Service Manager.

That makes it six jobs each: much more equitable. Anyone should be able to do six jobs on an average day. The organization is done!

Not a bit of work had been performed on the job, and yet the two of them were able to conceive of the company; the work that needs to be done; the standards by which they would hold each position accountable; and which position is accountable to which position and specifically for what.

And upon completing this one preparatory act, a sense of order swept through Jack and Murray. A sense of elation. For despite the obvious size of the job ahead, somehow it looked doable. Somehow they knew they were going to get it all done. They were organized. They had a plan.

**Widget Makers, Inc.
Organization Chart,
Version II**

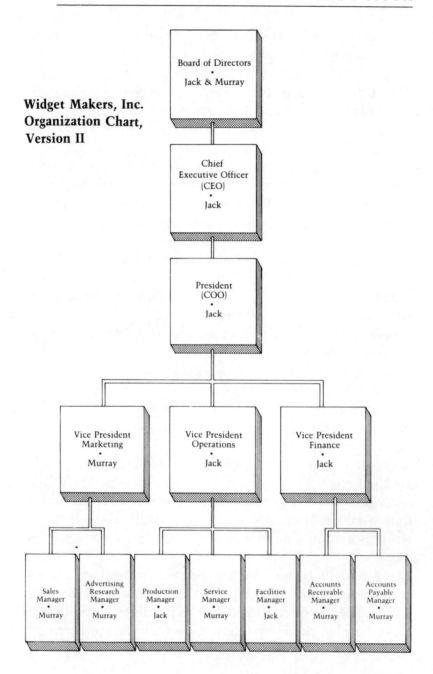

For with the creation of their Organization Chart, Jack and Murray had also generated the blueprint for their Franchise Prototype.

Prototyping the Position: Replacing Yourself with a System

Having created a picture of the business as it will look when it's finally done, Jack and Murray start the prototyping process. But at the *bottom* of the organization, not at the top.

They start prototyping the business where they start working in the business. In the position of Salesperson and Production person and Accounts Receivable Clerk. Not as the CEO or the COO or the VP/Marketing. Not as owners or partners or shareholders. But as *employees.* At the very bottom of the organization. Doing Tactical Work, not Strategic Work.

Tactical Work is the work all technicians do. Strategic Work is the work their managers do. If Jack and Murray's business is going to thrive, they have to find other people to do the Tactical Work so as to free Jack and Murray to do the Strategic Work.

The Organization Chart is the means through which that critical transition can be made.

Let's watch as Jack and Murray go through the same growth process they experienced at the beginning of this chapter, but this time avoiding their earlier disaster by prototyping the positions in their Organization Chart.

Jack and Murray go to work in their business. But now with a difference. They are no longer interested in *working in their business.* They are now focused on *developing a business that works.*

To do that they begin to work in an entirely different way.

As Murray goes to work *in* the position of Salesperson, he also goes to work *on* the position of Salesperson as Vice President/Marketing.

As Jack goes to work *in* the position of Production Person, he also goes to work *on* the position of Production Person as Vice President/Operations.

In other words, Murray and Jack start building their business by looking at each *position* in the business *as though it were a Franchise Prototype of its own.*

As Murray goes to work *in* the position of Salesperson as a Salesperson, he goes to work *on* the position by implementing the Business Development Process of Innovation, Quantification, and Orchestration.

Likewise, when Jack goes to work *in* the position of Production Person as a Production Person, he goes to work *on* the position by implementing the Business Development Process of Innovation, Quantification, and Orchestration.

Each of them asks, "What would best serve our customer here? How could I most easily give the customer what he wants while also maximizing profits for the company? And at the same time, how could I give the person accountable for that work the best possible experience?"

Murray begins to test the clothing he wears as a Salesperson to see what colors and styles produce the greatest positive impact on the customers. He starts testing different words. He begins to think about how Widget Makers, Inc. interacts with its customers, and how each component of this interaction could be modified to increase its effectiveness.

And as he quantifies the impact of his innovations on

sales, he takes the most productive of them and writes them down in the Widget Makers Sales Operations Manual.

Before long, the Manual contains the exact scripts for handling incoming calls, outgoing calls, meeting the customer at the door. The exact responses to customer inquiries, complaints, concerns. The system by which an order is entered, returns are transacted, new product requests are acted upon, inventory is secured.

Only when the Sales Operations Manual is complete does Murray run an ad for a salesperson. But not for someone with sales experience. Not a Master Technician. But a novice. A beginner. Someone eager to learn how to do it right. Someone willing to learn what Murray has spent so much time and energy discovering. Someone for whom questions haven't become answers. Someone who is open to the possibility of learning.

And the ad is placed in the Sales Section of the Sunday paper. It reads, "COME AND SEE OUR TURN-KEY OPERATION. COME AND SEE OUR MONEY MACHINE. NO EXPERIENCE NECESSARY. JUST AN OPEN MIND AND A WILLINGNESS TO LEARN."

And as Murray interviews the candidates, he shows them the Sales Operations Manual and Widget Makers' Strategic Objective and explains how they were created, and why. He shows them the Organization Chart, where the position of Salesperson is, to which position it reports, and who in Widget Makers is currently accountable for that position. He talks to them about their Primary Aim to determine who among them has a vision that coincides with Widget Makers' view of the world.

And when he finds the right person, Murray hires him, hands him the Sales Operations Manual, has him memorize the words in it, dress to code, learn the systems, and finally, go to work. *Using the Sales System Murray innovated, quantified, and orchestrated.*

At that moment, at that exact instant, Murray moves up to the position of Sales Manager *and begins the process of Business Development all over again.*

Because at that moment Murray has taken the most important step in freeing himself from the Tactical Work of his business. Murray has replaced himself with a *system* that works in the hands of a person who wants to work it.

And now Murray's job becomes managing the system rather than doing the work. Murray is now engaged in Strategic Work.

■ ■

Your Organization Chart flows down from your Strategic Objective, which in turn flows down from your Primary Aim. Each is the cause of the one preceding it, and each, therefore, plays a part in the fulfillment of the one before it. A logic is established, an integrated whole.

In this illustration, Widget Makers, Inc. became an orderly system for creating and recreating Jack and Murray's lives. Without the Organization Chart, confusion, discord, and conflict became the order of the day. But with it, the direction, purpose, and style of the business were suddenly balanced, interacting purposefully and progressing with intention and integrity toward a cohesive and sensible whole.

Finally, good people could come together and get something done!

15

YOUR MANAGEMENT STRATEGY

"The System is the Solution."

AT&T

You may think that the successful implementation of a Management Strategy is dependent upon finding amazingly competent managers—people with finely honed "people skills," with degrees from management schools, with highly sophisticated techniques for dealing with and developing their people.

It doesn't. You don't need such people. Nor can you afford them. They will be the bane of your existence. What you need, instead, is a Management System.

The *System* will become your strategy, the means through which your Franchise Prototype produces the results you want. The *System* will become your solution to the problems that beset you because of the unpredictability of your people. The *System* will transform your people problem into an opportunity by orchestrating the process by which management decisions are made, while at the same time eliminating the need for such decisions wherever and whenever possible.

What is a Management System? *It is a system designed into your Prototype to produce a marketing result.* And the more automatic that System is, the more effective your Franchise Prototype will be.

Management Development—the process through which you create your Management System—isn't a *management* tool as many people believe. It's a *marketing* tool. Its purpose is not to create an *efficient* Prototype but an *effective* one.

And an effective Prototype is a business that finds and keeps customers—profitably—better than any other.

Let's look at how such a system was put into practice by a resort hotel I've patronized over the past several years.

A Match, a Mint, a Cup of Coffee, and a Newspaper

The first time it was an accident; that is, an accident for me. I hadn't planned to go there.

I'd been driving for seven hours and, tired of the road, decided to stop for the night before going on to San Francisco. The hotel was located in a redwood grove overlooking the Pacific. By the time I walked into the lobby, the sun was setting and the grove had turned dark as pitch.

Instantly something told me that I was in a special place.

The lobby was warmly lighted. Redwood paneling reflected the red glow of the light onto beige overstuffed couches that hugged the three walls surrounding the reception desk. A long, dark wood table faced the front door through which I had just entered. On the table rested a huge woven Indian basket overflowing with fresh fruit. Beside the basket stood a massive bronze lamp, its deep burnished light bouncing off the fruit, adding a festive look to the room. Running the full length of the table and falling down on either end almost to the floor was an intricately crocheted linen cloth, its bright, exotic pattern accentuating the colors of the fruit, the bronze of the lamp, and the deep red ochre of the walls.

At the far side of the table, against the far wall, in a massive fieldstone fireplace, a roaring fire filled the room with the cheerful crackling of its furiously burning oak logs.

Even if I hadn't been so tired, the contrast between the heat of the flames on my face and the cold of the night at my back would have been enough to attract me to the room. As it was, I practically melted with delight.

Behind the reception desk a woman appeared dressed in a freshly starched red, green, and white gingham blouse and a deep red ochre skirt. A pin with the logo of the hotel atop a red ochre ribbon decorated her blouse like a badge of honor. A matching ribbon held her hair back from a glowing face.

"Welcome to Venetia," she smiled warmly.

It took no more than three minutes from the moment she spoke that greeting to the time the bellboy ushered me into my room, despite the fact that I had no reservation. I couldn't believe the ease with which it all happened.

And the room! The overall impression was one of understated opulence—thick, muted pastel wall-to-wall carpeting; a four-poster, king-size white pine bed covered by a magnificent, impeccably clean, white-on-white quilt; original graphics depicting scenes and birds of the Pacific Northwest gracing the rough-hewn elegance of the natural cedar walls; a stone fireplace with oak logs already prepared and waiting on the grate for the fire someone knew I would appreciate, paper rolled ceremoniously beneath the grate, and an elegant over-sized match lying diagonally across the hearth, waiting to be struck.

Delighted with my good fortune, I changed for dinner (the woman at the desk had made my reservation when she checked me in), and walked out into the night to find the restaurant. A sign by a path outside of my room pointed me down another well-lit path through the dark redwood grove. The night air was still and clear. In the distance I could hear the hushed, rhythmic patter of the Pacific Ocean surf. Or was it my imagination? It scarcely mattered; an aura of magic surrounded the place.

The restaurant stood on a knoll overlooking the hotel and the ocean. Until I went inside, I hadn't seen another person, but the restaurant was crowded. I gave the *maitre d'* my name and he immediately showed me to a table, despite the fact that other people were waiting. Evidently, reservations meant something in this restaurant!

The meal was as delightful as everything I had experienced before it, the food attractively prepared, the service attentive yet unobtrusive. I lingered over a glass of brandy while enjoying a classical guitarist who played a selection of Bach fugues for the dinner guests.

I signed the check and returned to my room, noting on the way that the lights had been turned up on the path apparently to compensate for the growing darkness. By the time I arrived at my room, the night had become chilly. I was looking forward to a fire and possibly another brandy before going to bed.

Somebody had beaten me to it!

A brisk fire was burning in the fireplace. The quilt was turned down on the bed. The pillows were plumped up, a mint resting on each one. On one of the night tables beside the bed stood a glass of brandy and a card. I picked up the card and read:

Welcome to your first stay at Venetia. I hope it has been enjoyable. If there is anything I can do for you, Day or night, please don't hesitate to call.
   Kathi

As I drifted to sleep that evening, I felt *very* well taken care of.

■ ■

The following morning I awoke to a strange bubbling sound in the bathroom. I arose to investigate. A pot of coffee, turned on by an automatic timer, was merrily perking away on the sink counter. A card resting against the pot said, "Your brand of coffee. Enjoy! K."

And it *was* my brand of coffee! How in the world could they have known that? And then I remembered. At the restaurant the night before they had asked me what brand of coffee I preferred. And here it was!

Just as I caught on to what they had done, there was a polite knock at the door. I went to the door and opened it. Nobody. But there on the mat was a newspaper. *My* newspaper, *The New York Times.* How in the world did they know that? And then I remembered. When I checked in the night before the receptionist had asked me what newspaper I preferred. I hadn't given it another thought. Until now. And there it was!

And exactly the same scenario has occurred each and every time I've returned.

But after that first time I was never asked my preferences again. I had become a part of the hotel's Management System. And never once has it let me down. The system knows what I like and makes certain that I get it, in exactly the same way, at exactly the same time.

What exactly had the System provided?

A match, a mint, a cup of coffee, and a newspaper!

But it wasn't the match, the mint, the cup of coffee or the newspaper that did it. *It was that somebody had heard me.* And they heard me *every single time!*

The moment I walked into the room and felt the fire, I knew that someone had thought about me. Had thought about what *I* wanted.

I hadn't said a word, and yet they had heard me.

The moment I saw the mints on the pillows, the turned down quilt, and the brandy on the table, I knew that someone had thought about me. Had thought about what *I* wanted.

I hadn't said a word and yet they had heard me.

The moment I heard the coffee pot perking in the bathroom and saw the card that identified it as my brand, I remembered that someone had asked for my preference.

And they had heard my answer.

The instant I saw the newspaper and recognized it as *my* newspaper, I remembered that someone had asked.

And they had heard my answer.

And it was totally automatic!

Every single element was an orchestrated solution designed to produce a marketing result, an integrated component of the hotel's Management System.

After my third visit to the hotel, I asked to speak with the Manager. I wanted to find out how he was able to produce the identical results for me every single time. How could he make certain that someone would ask the right questions so as to ensure the correct results for each and every guest? Was it because he hired extremely competent people? Were the employees owners? Was it some kind of special incentive system?

The Manager was a young man of twenty-nine. He invited me into his office to talk. It was well-lit, modest in size, and overlooked the redwood grove I had walked through to get to the restaurant. His desk was clean and neatly organized, not a loose paper in sight.

"This is a very orderly young man," I thought to myself. "Perhaps *he's* the reason the hotel works so well."

He obviously enjoyed his job, because he warmed immediately to the conversation about his work and the task of producing the results for which he was held accountable by the hotel's owner.

"You know," he said, smiling self-consciously, "it's funny sitting here talking to you about what we do here at the hotel. Because until five months ago, the only experience I had in the hotel business was as a guest for two nights at a Holiday Inn in Fresno three years ago. In fact," he continued, "before this job I was working as a short order cook at a restaurant nearby. The owner and I got to know each other. He asked if I'd like to learn the hotel business and, before I knew it, he hired me. Everything I know about the hotel business I've learned here.

"Here, let me show you."

He reached behind his desk for a red binder. Printed on the spine were the initials OM and the logo of the hotel.

"What we do here is simple. Anyone can do it."

He opened the binder to the table of contents.

"This is our Operations Manual. As you can see, it's nothing but a series of checklists. This one is a checklist on setting up a room." He opened the book to a yellow page.

"This group of pages is yellow. Everything in the Manual is color coded. Yellow has to do with Room Set Up. Blue, with Guest Support Services. For instance, when we light your fire at night, put the mints on your pillow, and so on.

"Each checklist itemizes the specific steps each Room

Support Person must take to do his or her job. There are eight packages of checklists for each Room Support Person waiting in their mailbox when they come in every day. Each package of checklists is used for one of the eight rooms the Room Support Person is accountable for.

"As a Room Support Person goes about the process of taking care of his or her eight rooms, a checklist is completed to confirm that each accountability was performed according to the standards. As you can see, here at the bottom of the checklist is a place for the RSP to sign, indicating that he or she did the prescribed work.

"To sign and not to have done the work is grounds for instant dismissal.

"But there's another part of the system that really makes it work.

"On the back of each checklist is a drawing of the specific room that identifies each task to be completed, and the order in which it has to be done. The drawing takes the RSP through the routine and, as they complete each task, they check off the corresponding part of the drawing to show that it was done.

"With this drawing we can train new people almost instantly, and have them producing a result identical to that of a person who's been with us for quite some time.

"As added insurance, my RSP Supervisors run spot checks every day to make certain that any errors are caught in time."

He paused and smiled. "But there are rarely any errors. The system works like a charm.

"There's an equally effective system for everything we do here. The fact is, the owner worked it all out in advance. The lighting, the sauna, and the pool are timed electronically and synchronized with the seasons, so that they deliver a predictable result to the guests. For example, you might have noticed that at night the outdoor lights increase in intensity as it gets darker. That's done automatically. No one has to think about it.

"I could give you lots of other examples, but I think you get the point. The whole thing was put together in a way the owner believed would make a positive impression on our guests. You'd be amazed at how many people come up to me after staying here just to thank me for how well they were treated.

"But it's not the *big* things they talk about, it's always the *little* things."

I could understand and believe all he had said, but still I asked, "How do you get your RSPs to use the checklists? How do you get them to use the system? Don't they get tired of the routine? Doesn't it get boring for them?"

"Ah," said my willing host.

"That's where we *really* shine."

16

YOUR PEOPLE STRATEGY

"Life games reflect life aims."

Robert S. DeRopp
The Master Game

"**H**ow do I get my people to do what I want?"
This is the one question I hear most often from business owners.

And the answer I give them is, "You can't! You can't *get* your people to do anything.

"If you want it done," I tell them, "you're going to have to create an environment in which 'doing it' is more important to your people than not doing it. Where 'doing it' well becomes a way of life for them."

Since that was the question most often asked of me, I was intrigued with the hotel Manager's answer to my question, "How do you get your people to do what you want?"

His response was refreshing because it was so atypical of small business people.

"The first thing that surprised me when I came to

work here," the Manager said, "was that *the owner took me seriously.*

"I mean, think about it. Here I was, a kid with absolutely no experience in this business. But he never treated me that way. He treated me as though I were a serious adult. Somebody worth talking to about what he obviously considered important.

"And that was the second thing that surprised me when I came to work here," the Manager continued. "How seriously the Boss took the operation of this hotel. I mean, it wasn't just that he took it seriously—everyone I've ever worked for was serious about his business—it was the *kind* of seriousness he had. It was as though the hotel was more than just a hotel to him. It was like the hotel was an expression of who *he* was, a symbol of what he believed in. So if I hadn't taken the hotel seriously, it would have looked like I wasn't taking *him* seriously, as a man whose values I respected.

"I guess that's why he took *me* seriously. It established a level of communication between us that made it possible for me to listen to what he believed in and how the hotel expressed those beliefs on a day-to-day basis.

"I'll never forget my first day here," he went on. "It was like I was being initiated into a fraternity or something. It was right here that it happened." He waved his arm in a circle indicating the office in which we were sitting. "This used to be his office.

"I was sitting where you're sitting," he said. "And the Boss was sitting here." He pointed at the chair in which he was sitting.

"It was a Monday morning and they had just had a big weekend, so there was a ton of stuff to do. Usually when I start on a new job, the first thing that happens is that the person who hires me takes a minute to describe what I'm

119

supposed to do, and then throws me out there to do it. So I was surprised when the Boss asked me if I wanted a cup of coffee. He seemed so unhurried, so *un*businesslike, you might say.

"No that wasn't it," the Manager corrected himself. "He was probably the *most* businesslike person I had ever met. But it was *how* he was about his business that struck me. He seemed to be saying that what we were going to talk about was the most important thing on his agenda that day, that discussing my job was more important to him than doing the work that was going on at the time. He wasn't hiring me to *work*, he was hiring me to do something much more important than that."

The Manager smiled. "You know, I've never said this to anyone before. It's really strange, but while I'm telling you all of this, it's becoming clear to me why I have so much respect for this place. It's because I have so much respect for the Boss. To me, the place is him. If I didn't respect him, I don't think I would be as good at what I do here as I am. Somehow the *idea* of what we do here is his idea. And that's what he took so long to communicate to me on that first day—his idea of this place. And what that meant to him.

"What he told me was something nobody has ever said to me before in any job. He said, 'The work we do is a reflection of who we are. If we're sloppy at it, it's because we're sloppy inside. If we're late at it, it's because we're late inside. If we're bored by it, it's because we're bored inside, with ourselves, not with the work. The meanest work can be a piece of art when done by an artist. So the job here is not *outside* of ourselves, but *inside* of ourselves. How we do our work becomes a mirror of how we are inside.' "

The Manager continued, as if the owner were talking

through him. "Work is passive without you. It can't do anything. Work is only an idea before a person does it. But the moment a person does it, the impact of the work on the world becomes a reflection of that idea—the idea behind the work—as well as the person doing it.

"In the process, the work you do becomes you. And you become the force that breathes life into the idea behind the work. You become the creator of the impact on the world of the work you do.

"There is no such thing as undesirable work. There are only people who see certain kinds of work as undesirable. People who use every excuse in the world to justify why they have to do work they hate to do. People who look upon their work as a punishment for who they are and where they stand in the world, rather than as an opportunity to see themselves as they really are.

"People like that don't bring life to the idea of the work they do, they bring death to it.

"The result is sloppy, inconsiderate, inconsistent, inhuman transactions between most businesses and the people who buy from them. Exactly the *opposite* of what we have here.

"And the reason it's different here is because we give everyone who comes to work at the hotel an opportunity to make a choice. Not *after* they've done the work, but before.

"And we do that *by making sure they understand the idea behind the work they're being asked to do.*

"I guess that's what excited me most about taking this job," said the Manager. "It's the very first place I've ever gone to work where *there was an idea behind the work that was more important than the work itself.*

"The idea the Boss expressed to me was broken down into three parts:

"The first says that the customer is not always right but whether he is or not, it is our job to make him feel that way.

"The second says that everyone who works here is expected to work toward being the best he can possibly be at the tasks he's accountable for. When he can't do that, he should act like he is until he gets around to it. And if he's unwilling to act like it, he should leave.

"The third says that the business is a place where everything we know how to do is tested by what we don't know how to do, and that the conflict between the two is what creates growth, what creates meaning.

"The idea the Boss has about the business comes down to one essential notion. That a business is like a martial arts practice hall, a *dojo,* a place you go to practice being the best you can be. But the true combat in a *dojo* is not between one person and another as most people believe it to be. The true combat in a martial arts practice hall is between the people *within ourselves.*

"That's what the Boss and I talked about in our first meeting. His philosophy about work and about business. I came to understand that the hotel was the *least* important thing in our relationship. What *was* important was how seriously I took to playing the game he had created here.

"He wasn't looking for employees so much as for players in his game. He was looking for people who wanted something more than just a job."

■ ■

People—your people—do not simply want to work for exciting people. They want to work for people who have created a clearly defined structure for acting in the world. A structure through which they can test themselves and be tested.

Such a structure is called a game. And there is nothing more exciting than a well-conceived game.

That is what the very best businesses represent to the people who create them. A game to be played in which the rules symbolize the idea you, the owner, have about the world. If your idea is a positive one, your business will reflect that optimism. If your idea is a negative one, your business will reflect that as well.

In this context, the degree to which your people "do what you want" is the degree to which they buy into your game. And the degree to which they buy into your game doesn't depend upon *them* but upon how well you communicate the game to them—at the *outset* of your relationship, not after it's begun.

Your People Strategy is the way you communicate this idea. It starts with your Primary Aim and your Strategic Objective, and continues through your Organizational Strategy (your Organization Chart and the Postition Contracts for all of the positions in it) and the Operations Manuals that define the work your people do.

It is communicated through the beliefs you have and the way you expect your Prototype to exemplify them; through the standards you establish for the performance of accountabilities at all levels and in all sectors of your Prototype; through the words you use to describe what your business needs to become—for your customer, for your people, for yourself—if it is to be more than just a place where people go to work.

But the game your business will play can't simply be deferred to the written page. It must be *seen* if it is to work. It must be experienced.

It is—first, last, and always—about how you *act.*

The words will become hollow if the game is a contrived one. The game can't be created as a device to enroll your people. It can't become cynical if it's to provide your people what they need in order to come alive while playing it. The game has to be real. You have to mean it.

The game is a measure of you.

How you act in the game establishes how you will be regarded by the other players.

The Rules of the Game

As in any game, there are rules for the People Game if you are to become any good at it. I've included a few here to give you a taste for them. As for the rest of them, you'll have to discover them for yourself by playing a game of your own. You'll learn the rules in the process.

1. **Never figure out what you want your people to do, and then try to create a game out of it.** If it's to be seen as serious, the game has to come first; what your people do, second.

2. **Never create a game for your people you're unwilling to play yourself.** They'll find you out and never let you forget it.

3. **Make sure there are specific ways of winning the game without ending it.** The game can never end because the end will take the life right out of your business. But unless there are victories in the process, your people will grow weary. Hence, the value of victories now and then. They keep people in the game and make the game appealing, even when it's not.

4. **Change the game from time to time—the tactics, *not* the strategy.** The strategy is its ethic, the moral underpinning of your game's logic. This must re-

main sacrosanct, for it is the foundation of you and your peoples' commitment to each other. But change is necessary. For any game can become ordinary, no matter how exhilarating it may be at the beginning.

To know when change is called for, watch your people. Their results will tell you when the game's all but over. The trick is to anticipate the end *before* anyone else does, and to change it by executive action. You'll know if you've pulled it off by watching how everyone responds to the change. Not at first. You can expect some resistance at first. But persist. Your persistence will move them through their resistance into your new and more enlivening game.

5. **Never expect the game to be self-sustaining. People need to be reminded of it constantly.** At least once a week create a special meeting about the Game. At least once a day, make some kind of issue about an exception to the way the game has been played— and make certain that everyone knows about it.

   Remember, in and of itself the game doesn't exist. It is alive to the degree that people make it so. But people have the unerring ability to forget everything they start, and to be distracted by trivia. Most great games are lost that way. To make certain yours isn't, don't expect your people to be something they're not. Remind them, time after time, of the game they're playing with you. You can't remind them too often.

6. **The game has to make sense.** an illogical game will abort before it ever gets going. The best games are built on universally verifiable truths. Everyone

should be able to see them if they're to be sufficiently attractive. A game with muddy beginnings will get you nowhere. Know the ground you stand on, and then assemble your armament. Sooner or later you'll need it. For a game that isn't tested isn't a game at all.

But remember, you can have the best reasons in the world for your game and still end up with a loser if the logic is not supported by a strong emotional commitment. All the logic does is give your people the rational armament to support their emotional commitment. If their commitment wanes, it means that they—and most likely, you—have forgotten the logic. So wheel out the logic often. Make sure everyone remembers the game's *raison d'etre*.

7. **The game needs to be fun from time to time.** Note that I said, *from time to time*. No game needs to be fun all the time. In fact, a game is often no fun at all. That's part of the thrill of playing a game well; learning how to deal with the "no fun" part so as to retain your dignity while falling on your face.

At the same time, fun needs to be planned into your game. But make certain that the fun you plan *is* fun. Employee picnics, baseball games, or cocktail parties could not only *not* be fun but be so stupid that they bring the entire game into question. Fun needs to be defined by your people. If it's fun to them, it will work. But not too often, maybe once every six months. Something to look forward to, and something to forget.

8. **If you can't think of a good game, steal one.** Anyone's ideas are as good as your own. But once you steal somebody else's game, learn it by heart.

There's nothing worse than pretending to play a game, not even no game at all.

The Logic of the Game

To the hotel Manager, the Boss's game was a good one, so he learned how to play it. It was a simple game, but effective. It was built upon the following logic:

Most people today are not getting what they want. Not from their jobs, not from their families, not from their religion, not from their government and, most important, not from themselves.

Something is missing in most of our lives.

Part of what's missing is purpose. Values. Worthwhile standards against which our lives can be measured. Part of what's missing is a game worth playing.

What's also missing is a sense of relationship. People suffer in isolation from one another. In a world without purpose, without meaningful values, what have we to share but our emptiness, the needy fragments of our superficial selves? As a result, most of us scramble about hungrily seeking distraction, in music, in television, in people, in drugs.

And most of all we seek things. Things to wear and things to do. Things with which to fill the emptiness. Things to shore up our eroding sense of self. Things to which we can attach meaning, significance, life. We've fast become a world of things. And most people are being buried in the profusion.

What most people need, then, is a place of community that has purpose, order, and meaning. A place in which *being* human is a prerequisite, but *acting* human is essential. A place where the generally disorganized thinking that pervades our culture becomes organized and clearly focused on a specific worthwhile result. A place where discipline and will become prized for what they are: the backbone of enterprise and action, of being what you are intentionally instead of accidentally. A place that replaces the home most of us have lost.

That's what a business can do. It can become that place of community. It can become that place where words such as integrity, intention, commitment, vision, and excellence can be used, not as nouns, but as verbs, as action steps in the process of producing a worthwhile result.

What kind of result? Giving your customer a sense that your business is a special place, created by special people, doing what they do in the best possible way. And all being done for the simplest, most human reason possible—because they're alive!

What other reason do you need?

Human beings are capable of performing extraordinary acts. Capable of going to the moon. Capable of creating the computer. Capable of building a bomb that can destroy us all. The least we should be able to do is to run a small business that works.

For if we can't do that, then what's the value of our grand ideas? What purpose do they serve but to alienate us from ourselves, from each other, from who we are?

Playing the Game

Thinking the way the hotel owner did, you can begin to construct a mental map of the game he created. His hotel became a world in which the sensory experiences of his customer were greeted by a profound dedication to cleanliness, beauty, and order.

But this dedication didn't rest on a purely commercial justification (though there was that too; no business could be successful without it) but a moral one. On the Boss's philosophy, his view of the world, his idea.

The idea was then communicated to his people, both in word and deed, through a well-planned process. The importance of this cannot be overstated. The Boss communicated his idea through documented systems *and* through his warm, moving, and positive manner. He knew that he could communicate the orderly yet human process of pleasing customers to his people only if it were communicated to them in an orderly and human way.

In short, the *medium* of communication became as important as the idea it was designed to communicate.

And the hotel's hiring process became the first and most essential medium for communicating the Boss's idea. As the Manager explained it to me, the hiring process was comprised of several distinct components.

1. A scripted presentation communicating the Boss's idea in a group meeting to all of the applicants at the same time. This presentation described not only the idea, but also the business's history and experience in successfully implementing that idea, and the attributes required of the successful candidate for the position in question.

2. Meeting with each applicant individually to discuss his reactions to and feelings about the idea, as well as his background and experience. At this meeting, each applicant was also asked why he felt he was superbly appropriate for the role the position was to play in implementing the Boss's idea.

3. Notification of the successful candidate by telephone. Again, a scripted presentation.

4. Notification of the unsuccessful applicants, thank-

ing each for his interest. A standard letter, signed by the interviewer.

5. First day of training to include the following activities for both the Boss and the new employee.

- Reviewing the Boss's idea;
- Summarizing the system through which the entire business brings the idea to reality;
- Taking the new employee on a tour of the facilities, highlighting people at work and systems at work to demonstrate the interdependence of the systems on people and the people on systems;
- Answering clearly and fully all the employee's questions;
- Issuing the employee his uniform and his Operations Manual;
- Reviewing the Operations Manual, including the Strategic Objective, the Organizational Strategy, the Position Contract of the employee's position; and,
- Completing his employment papers.

And the hiring process is just the beginning! Just think. All of this simply to *start* a relationship!

Are you beginning to understand that systematizing your business need not be a dehumanizing experience, but quite the opposite?

That in order to get your people to do what you want, *you'll first have to create an environment that will make it possible?*

That hiring people, developing people, and keeping people requires a strategy built upon an understanding of people completely foreign to most businesses?

That the system is indeed the solution?

That *without* an idea worth pursuing, there can be no People Strategy at all?

But *with* that idea you can finally say, just as our young Manager said, "That's where we really shine!"

17

YOUR MARKETING STRATEGY

"What we have here is a failure to communicate."

Anonymous

I've already said it: your Marketing Strategy starts, ends, lives, and dies with your customer.

So in the development of your Marketing Strategy it is absolutely imperative that you forget about your dreams, forget about your visions, forget about your interests, forget about what *you* want—forget about everything but your customer!

When it comes to Marketing, what *you* want is unimportant.

It's what your customer wants that matters.

And what your customer wants is significantly different from what you *think* he wants.

The Irrational Decisionmaker

Try to visualize your customer. He's standing before you. He's not frowning, nor is he smiling. He is perfectly neutral.

Yet, there's something strange about him.

Coming out of his forehead, reaching up toward the ceiling, is an antenna! And at the end of the antenna is a sensor, beeping away like crazy.

And the sensor is taking in all of the sensory data around it—the colors, shapes, sounds, and smells of your store, or your office, or the restaurant where you're meeting for lunch. It's also taking in sensory data from *you:* how you are standing or sitting, the color of your hair, how your hair is combed, the expression on your face—is it tense, are you looking directly at him or off to the side— the crease in your slacks, the color of your shoes—are they shined, worn, are the laces tied?

Nothing escapes the sensor as it absorbs the stimuli from the environment. Nothing escapes your customer as he absorbs the information he uses to make his decision to buy or not to buy.

But this step in the buying process is only the first. It's what the sensor *does* with the information that's of interest here. Because it's how the sensor processes the information that will determine the decision your customer is about to make.

Think of the sensor as your customer's Conscious Mind. Its job is to gather up the information needed for a decision. Most of what it does, however, is unconscious; that is, automatic, habitual. So even though your customer's Conscious Mind is actively absorbing all manner and forms of impressions, it is *totally unaware* of most of them. It can do it—literally—in its sleep. In fact, it can't *stop* doing it!

Fortunately, the Conscious Mind doesn't need to be aware. For the Conscious Mind doesn't have to make a decision.

133

The decision is made by your customer's *Un*conscious Mind.

It's in your customer's Unconscious Mind where all the action is. Where the second step of the buying process takes place.

Where is your customer's Unconscious Mind?

It's like a vast, dark, underground sea in which a multitude of exotic creatures swim about, single and in schools, silently seeking out food, each with entirely different needs and tastes.

Those creatures are your customer's expectations.

And in the sea in which they swim is a truly foreign place to your customer. He has no idea what's swimming around down there. What's lurking behind some subterranean rock. What's lying still and quiet as a stone on the bottom, waiting patiently and deliberately for some sweet morsel to wander by.

But every creature in that sea—every one of those expectations—is a product of your customer's life!

Of his reactions, perceptions, attitudes, associations, beliefs, opinions, inferences, conclusions. An accumulation of all his experiences since the instant of his birth (and for all we know, before it) to this very moment when he stands before you.

And all his expectations are nothing more or less than the means through which the sum of them all—your customer's *personality*—gets fed what *it* needs.

The food it needs comes in the form of sensory input from the Conscious Mind (the "surface"). And if the food is compatible with its expectations, the Unconscious Mind says, "Yes." And if the food is incompatible with its expectations, the Unconscious Mind says, "No."

And the decision, yes or no, is made at the *instant* it gets a taste!

134

In a television commercial, the sale is made or lost in the first *three or four seconds.*[1]

In a print ad, 75 percent of the buying decisions are made *at the headline alone.*[2]

In a sales presentation, the sale is made or lost *in the first three minutes.*[3]

And all that happens *after* that psychographic moment of truth, *after* the buying decision is made, is that the Unconscious Mind sends its answer up to the Conscious Mind, which then goes back out into the world to assemble the rational armament to support its already determined emotional commitment.

And that's how buying decisions are made.

Irrationally!

No one has ever made a rational decision to buy anything!

So when your customer says, "I want to think about it," *don't believe him.* He's *not* going to think about it. *He doesn't know how.* He's already done all the "thinking" he's going to do—he either wants it or not.

What your customer is really saying is one of two things: he is either emotionally incapable of saying no for fear of how you might react if he told you the truth, or you haven't provided him with the "food" his Unconscious Mind craves.

Either way, *little or no thought enters into the transaction.* The decision was made unconsciously and instantaneously. In fact, it was made long before you ever met.

But your customer didn't know it.

---

1. John Caples, *Tested Advertising Methods* (Englewood Cliffs, NJ; Prentice-Hall, Inc., 1974).
2. Ibid.
3. Ibid.

The Two Pillars of a Successful Marketing Strategy

The question then becomes, "If my *customer* doesn't know what he wants, how can *I?*"

The answer is, you can't!

Not unless you know more about him than he does about himself. Not unless you know his demographics and his psychographics.

Demographics and psychographics are the two essential pillars supporting a successful marketing program. If you know *who* your customer is (demographics), you can then determine *why he buys* (psychographics). And having done so, you can begin to construct a Prototype to satisfy his unconscious needs, *scientifically*, rather than arbitrarily.

Again, demographics is the science of marketplace reality. It tells you *who* buys. Psychographics is the science of *perceived* marketplace reality. It tells you why certain demographic types buy for one reason while other demographic types buy for another.

Let me give you an example of how these sciences might be utilized in your Marketing Strategy.

Notice the shade of blue on the jacket of this book. I call it "IBM Blue." Why? Because it's IBM's color. (That's why, I imagine, IBM is called "Big Blue" in the marketplace.) Why that specific shade of blue rather than another? Why blue at all? Because that shade of blue has an extraordinarily high appeal and preference to IBM's Central Demographic Model. They see that shade of blue, and it's love at first sight! Ever heard the expression, "True Blue?" That's what that particular color is: the color IBM's Central Demographic Model consumer *knows* it can depend on.

What would have happened had IBM chosen orange instead of blue?

Well, since orange is at the opposite end of the preferential spectrum for IBM's consumer, the IBM success story may not have been so momentous. Their consumer would have had trouble buying an orange computer!

Now, I know that sounds ridiculous, but you can test it if you like.

Remember the little test I suggested earlier in this book, the one with the navy blue suit? I'd like you to visualize someone wearing such a suit. Can you see him in your mind's eye? Deep navy blue, vested, possibly a pin stripe. Sharply creased trousers. White starched shirt. A red and blue striped tie. Black, highly polished wing-tip shoes.

Now how do you feel about him? Does he look businesslike? Does he look like someone you can trust? Does he appear to represent something solid, reliable, dependable?

Of course he does.

Research shows that the navy suit is perhaps the most powerful suit a person can wear in business. Instant impact.

It's been said that Charles Revson, the founder of Revlon, owned 220 suits—*all navy blue!* He knew what worked.

Now visualize the very same person you did before, but this time he's not wearing a navy blue suit.

Now he's wearing . . . *an orange suit.*

That's right, a three-piece orange suit! An expensive one at that. And with it, he's wearing a white-on-white silk shirt and a green and white striped Italian silk tie. And a silver belt buckle with his initials in green jade across its face. And a diamond tie pin, two carat, glimmering out at

137

you just above the top button of his vest. And a pair of white lizard cowboy boots.

Get the picture?

Well, take it fast *because he's out of business.*

The difference between the two men isn't in *them,* it's in your *mind.* Your Unconscious mind. What's more, the difference is perceived instantly without a moment of thought.

The fact that you couldn't conduct serious business with the man in the orange suit but you could if he were wearing blue says that *there is no such thing as reality.*

Reality only exists in someone's perceptions, attitudes, beliefs, conclusions—whatever you wish to call those positions of the mind from which all expectations arise—*and nowhere else.*

So the famous dictum which says, "Find a need and fill it" is, in fact, inaccurate. It should say, "Find a *perceived* need and fill it." Because if your customer doesn't *perceive* he needs something, he doesn't, even if he actually *does.* Get it?

Those perceptions are at the heart of your customer's decisionmaking process. And if you know his demographics you can understand what those perceptions are, and then figure out what you must do to satisfy them and the expectations they produce. You can know your customer's psychographic reality.

Each demographic model has a specific set of perceptions that are identifiable in advance. Women of a certain age, with a certain amount of education, with a certain size family, living in a certain geography, buy for very specific psychographic reasons. Those unconsciously held reasons will be different from another group of women, of a different age and marital status, with a different educational background, living in a different part of the country.

And these differences predetermine what each group buys.

Are you beginning to get a sense of the complexity of this business called Marketing? I hope so. Because until you do, until you begin to take it seriously, until you give it the earnest attention it demands, your Prototype will continue to be the only thing it could hope to be under the circumstances—a crap shoot!

At The Michael Thomas Corporation, we have created tools for our small-business clients to begin the often arduous task of making demographic and psychographic determinations, and how to position their Prototype in the mind of their consumer.

The impact has been astonishing.

Small businesses that acted like small businesses when we met them began to operate with intelligence. Their customers came vividly alive to them, often for the very first time. Inquiry, the active solicitation of specific information, and controlled experimentation replaced the guessing, blind hope, and feverish busy work that preceded them. Innovation, Quantification and Orchestration became the driving forces behind their efforts.

The fact is, any small business can do it. And every small business must!

If Mature businesses, such as IBM, Proctor & Gamble, and McDonald's take such things seriously, then how can you not do the same? Your business is far more fragile than a big business. So if anything, you must take Marketing *more* seriously than a big business does.

And time is running out.

We have entered the "unforgiving age." An age in which countless small businesses will either accept the challenge of an information-glutted society or be destroyed by it. An age in which your customer is deluged by so many products and promises that he becomes swamped in confusion and indecision.

The challenge of our age is to learn your customer's language. And then to speak that language clearly and well so that your voice can be heard above the din.

Because if your customer doesn't hear you, he'll pass you by.

■ ■

No doubt you feel frustrated as you read this. You must be asking yourself, "How do I do it? How do I determine my customer's demographics, his psychographics? What colors to use? What shapes? What words?"

But if you're asking those questions, you're well on your way! For the purpose of this book is not to *answer* those questions, but to *provoke* them! Not "how-to-do-it," but "what-needs-to-be-done."

Unless you understand what-needs-to-be-done; unless you understand the essential importance of Marketing to your Prototype; unless you understand that your customer is far less rational in his convictions and expectations than you had ever imagined; unless you understand that your Prototype is your product; all the how-to-do-it in the world won't make a bit of difference to you.

But we're not finished yet.

We have one more step to take in your Business Development Program.

Your Systems Strategy, the glue that holds your Prototype together.

18

YOUR SYSTEMS STRATEGY

"The world thus appears as a complicated tissue of events, in which connections of different kinds alternate or overlap or combine and thereby determine the texture of the whole."

Werner Heisenberg
Physics and Philosophy

Throughout this book I have talked about systems without really defining what a system is.

A system is a set of things, actions, ideas, and information that interact with each other, and in so doing alter other systems.

In short, *everything* is a system. The universe, the world, San Francisco Bay, the office I'm sitting in, the word processor I'm using, the cup of coffee I'm drinking, the relationship you and I are having—they're all systems.

Some systems we can understand and some we can't. Let's look at the ones we can. The systems in your business.

Three Kinds of Systems

There are three kinds of systems in your business: Hard Systems, Soft Systems, and Information Systems.

Hard Systems are inanimate, unliving things. My word processor is a Hard System, as are the colors in this office's reception area.

Soft Systems are either animate—living—or ideas. You are a Soft System; so is the script for *Hamlet.*

Information Systems are those that provide us with information about the interaction between the other two. Inventory control, cash flow forecasting, sales activity are all Information Systems.

The Innovation, Quantification, Orchestration, and *integration* of these three kinds of systems in your business is what your Business Development Program is all about.

What follows are examples of each, and how they integrate to produce a desirable result.

Hard Systems

At The Michael Thomas Corporation, we use "black boards" extensively in seminars, internal meetings, and conferences with clients and prospective clients.

As you've probably guessed by now, our facilities are operated under rigid standards of color and cleanliness. Color standards dictate that we use *white* boards, rather than black ones, and blue markers, rather than white chalk. Unfortunately, our color standards also dictate that our walls be white.

It wasn't long before a conflict developed between our standards of cleanliness and our standards of color.

At the end of a seminar, a meeting, or a conference,

the person accountable for that particular event is to leave the room in the order in which he found it. This includes cleaning the board—work our people are not particularly fond of doing.

Not that they *wouldn't* do it; they would. But in their haste to get it done so they could get on with the work they preferred to do, the eraser would often fly uncontrollably over the edge of the board.

It wasn't long before our once gleaming white walls began to show ugly streaks and smudges of IBM-blue ink! It drove us crazy. We mounted an all-out campaign. We held Blue Ink On the Walls Meetings. We wrote memos entitled:

> *TO: All Personnel.*
> *SUBJECT: Blue Ink on Walls.*

We created new Board Cleaning Policies. We created Cleaning Teams. We created Wall Tours. We created Board Spot Checks. We installed signs above every board saying: BE CAREFUL!

But no matter what we did, no matter how hard we tried, no matter what we said to our normally meticulous people—blue ink got on the walls. Our only apparent recourse was to paint the walls white over and over again or go back to black boards and white chalk.

Neither was acceptable.

And that's how our Prevent-a-Smudge System was born.

We had one standard that insisted upon impeccably clean walls and another standard that made the first one seemingly impossible to uphold (white boards, white walls, blue ink). In short, we had a conflict between what we *wanted* and what we *had.*

143

The two necessary components of conflict.

The essential conditions for innovation.

The conditions that give birth to a system.

But a third component is needed to translate conflict into remedial action: *will.*

We were determined to lick the problem, and would not rest until we did.

Will applied to any conflict creates energy. Conflict without will creates frustration. An engine turning, but going nowhere. Conflict with will creates resolution, a movement beyond the dilemma.

Voila! The Michael Thomas Prevent-a-Smudge System!

It was so obvious. So simple.

We installed a clear lucite collar around each board.

Extending four inches out from each edge of the board, the lucite collar literally *stopped* the blue ink carnage in its tracks!

In one fell swoop, the walls were clean. Our people were delighted; the clients amazed. The constant painting, memo writing, sign creating, team invading, policy polluting activities that had pervaded our organization for more than three weeks was history.

And all because of a four-inch lucite collar!

A Hard System for producing a human and totally integrated result.

A system-solution to a typically people-intensive problem.

And it's working even now, at this very moment, without anyone having to pay attention to it. Leaving me free to write this book, or anything else I care to do.

That's the purpose of a system—to free you to do the things you want to do.

Soft Systems

Things need to be sold.

And it's usually people who have to sell them.

Everyone in business has heard the old saw: 80 percent of our sales are produced by 20 percent of our people. Unfortunately, few seem to know what the 20 percent are doing that the 80 percent aren't.

Well, let me tell you.

The 20 percent are using a system, and the 80 percent aren't.

A selling system is a Soft System.

And I've seen such systems produce 100 percent to 500 percent increases in sales in almost no time!

What is a selling system? It's a fully orchestrated interaction between you and your customer that follows five primary steps:

- identification of the specific Benchmarks—or consumer decision points—in your selling process;
- the *literal* scripting of the words that will get you to each one successfully (yes, written down like the script for a play!);
- the creation of the various materials to be used with each script;
- the *memorization* of each Benchmark's script;
- the delivery of each script by your salespeople in identical fashion.

At The Michael Thomas Corporation, we call it the Power Selling System.

A career development company we worked with put it in the hands of people with no experience, and revenues increased 300 percent in one year.

An advertising agency put it in the hands of people with no experience in either selling *or* advertising, and revenues increased 500 percent in two years.

A health spa put it in the hands of people with no experience, and revenues increased 40 percent—in *two months*.

If you put it to work in *your* company, it will do the same for you, no matter what kind of business you're in.

The Power Selling System is comprised of two parts: Structure and Substance. Structure is *what* you do. Substance is *how* you do it.

The Structure of the System includes exactly what you say, the materials you use when you say it, and what you wear.

The Substance of the System includes how you say it, how you use it when you say it, and how you *are* when you say it.

Structure and Substance merge in the selling process to produce a far more extraordinary result than any single salesperson could if left to his own devices.

Let's look more specifically at the most important component of the Power Selling System—what you say. Or what we call at MTC, the Power Selling Process.

The Power Selling Process

The Power Selling Process is actually a series of scripts defining the entire interaction between the salesperson and the customer.

These scripts (or Benchmarks) are:

1. The Appointment Presentation
2. The Needs Analysis Presentation
3. The Solutions Presentation

THE APPOINTMENT PRESENTATION   Most sales-people fail at the outset of the selling process because they don't realize the purpose of an Appointment Presentation. Most believe that the purpose of an Appointment Presentation is to qualify the customer and ascertain whether or not he is a viable prospect. It's not. The purpose of an Appointment Presentation is one thing and one thing only: *to make an appointment.*

The Appointment Presentation moves the prospect from where he is to the second Benchmark in the process, the Needs Analysis Presentation. It is a series of words, delivered on the telephone or in person, that engage the prospect's *unconscious* (remember?) by speaking primarily about the *product* you have to sell rather than the *commodity.*

For example:

> *"Hi, Mr. Jackson. I'm Johnny Jones with Walter Mitty & Company. Have you seen the remarkable new things that are being done to control money these days?"*
>
> *"What new things?"*
>
> *"Well, that's exactly why I called. May I have a moment of your time?"*

The product? Financial control. Control is the key. The presentation tells Mr. Jackson that there are things going on in the world ("remarkable new things") that he doesn't know about (he's out of control), but he can now become familiar with (gain control) by just spending a few moments with the salesperson.

And it tells him that instantly! Mr. Jackson's emotional commitment is already made. All that he needs now is to find the rational armament to support it. That's what the salesperson's job is. That's why the appointment will be made.

Simple and effective. It makes appointments.

To do what? To deliver the Needs Analysis Presentation.

THE NEEDS ANALYSIS PRESENTATION   The first thing you do in a Needs Analysis Presentation is repeat what you said in the Appointment Presentation to reestablish the emotional commitment:

> *"Remember, Mr. Jackson, when we first talked I mentioned that some remarkable new things were going on in the world to control money?"*

The second thing you do is tell the prospect how you would like to proceed to fulfill your promise to him:

> *"Well, what I'd like to do is to tell you about those things. At the same time, I'd like to show you some incredibly effective ways my firm, Walter Mitty & Company, has developed to help you to control money here in your business. OK?"*

The third thing you do is to establish your credibility in the prospect's mind by communicating two things. First, your company's expertise in such matters: "We are Money Controlling Specialists" (we call that a Positioning Statement). And second, your personal willingness to do whatever is necessary to utilize that expertise on his behalf:

> *"Let me tell you why we created our company, Mr. Jackson. We've found that people like yourself are continually frustrated by not being able to get the most out of their money. Frustrated by paying higher*

*interest rates than they have to. By working with finan-
cial experts who don't seem to know what they're
doing. By banking with a bank that doesn't seem to
have their best interest at heart. And so on.*

*"Do these things ever frustrate you, Mr. Jackson? Of
course they do. And that's why Walter Mitty & Company has created a Money Controlling System that
makes it possible for you to get the most preferential
treatment in the financial arena, while at the same time
paying the least for it. Now I know that sounds too good
to be true. But let me explain how we propose to go
about doing that for you. . . . "*

Here you're communicating that you understand what
frustrates Mr. Jackson, and that you have the expertise to
alleviate those frustrations—not *personally,* mind you, but
systemically—through the use of the Walter Mitty & Company Money Controlling System.

The fourth thing you do in a Needs Analysis Presentation is describe the Walter Mitty & Company Money Controlling System and why it works so well. Not *what* it does,
but the *impact it will have* on the prospect:

*"The Walter Mitty & Company Controlling System
is designed to do three things, Mr. Jackson.*

*"First, it enables us to know what specifically bothers
you about controlling your money. Because we know
that controlling money must be personally tailored to
each and every one of our clients. In order to do that
we've created what we call at Walter Mitty & Company a Money Management Questionnaire. By asking
you these particular questions, we're well on our way
to helping you get what you want. Before I leave today,
I'll review the Questionnaire with you.*

"Once the questionnaire is completed, we return it to our Financial Systems Group. This is a group of financial specialists who review your questionnaire to make certain that it has been completed accurately.

"If it has, they enter the information into our Money Controlling System which has been designed to analyze this information and compare it with the broad spectrum of data we've assembled over the years. Once having analyzed the information, the System will then create personally tailored solutions just for you, Mr. Jackson. Ways to secure the kind of preferential treatment we talked about earlier, but at the lowest possible cost. Ways of controlling your money and using it to your advantage, not someone else's.

"These solutions will then be prepared in the form of a Financial Report which I'll deliver to you personally and review with you at that time.

"Should any of our solutions make sense to you, we'll be more than happy to help you implement them. If not, then at least we'll have started the process of becoming better acquainted so that we may be of assistance to you some other time.

"In any case, the Financial Report is yours—at absolutely no cost whatsoever. It's our way of saying we're serious about what we do, and would be happy to work with you, whether now or in the future.

"So let's review the Questionnaire together, and when we're done I'll provide you with a summary of some of the remarkable new things that are happening in the world to control money. And then I'll take your information back so we can prepare your Financial Report. OK?"

The fifth thing you do in the Needs Analysis Presentation is complete the Money Management Questionnaire.

The sixth thing you do is provide the prospective customer with the information you promised him and show him how relevant it is to the Financial Report you will be preparing for him. (You could have done this at the outset of your meeting, during the Needs Analysis questioning process, or now, at the end.)

The seventh thing you do in the Needs Analysis Presentation is make an appointment with the prospective customer to return with the Financial Report, reminding him that you will have some valuable solutions for him— at no cost!—and that you will take whatever time is necessary to help him understand those solutions, whether he decides to implement them or not!

Upon completion of the Needs Analysis Presentation, you have made an appointment that will bring you to the third Benchmark in the Power Selling Process, the Solutions Presentation.

THE SOLUTIONS PRESENTATION   The Solutions Presentation is the easiest component of the Power Selling Process. Because if you have you done your job effectively up to this point *the sale is already made.*

Most salespeople think that selling is "closing." It isn't. Selling is *opening.* That's what the Needs Analysis Presentation does. It opens the prospective customer up to a deeper experience of his frustration and to the opportunities available to him by going through the questioning process with you.

You now have something to give him.

"Remarkable new things" that will make it possible for him to receive "preferential treatment" in the "financial arena" so as to secure the kind of "control" over his money he "deserves" and at a "preferentially" low cost.

In other words, by knowing you your prospective customer is going to (1) be on the inside of the financial winners circle with people who are in the know; (2) be treated like important people are; (3) use money like the "pros" do; and (4) gain control over his life. And he's going to get all of this without paying too high a price for it!

What more could anyone ask for?

The Solutions Presentation simply provides the rational armament for the emotional commitment (remember that?). Here you bring the prospect up-to-date by reviewing *everything* you said and did during the Needs Analysis Presentation. He's forgotten all those psychographically compelling things by now. But he won't for long—*they're a part of him.*

Then you review in great, patient, and earnest detail every last word, comma, and number in your prospective customer's Financial Report! You ask questions to make certain that he feels that this is *his* Financial Report, *not* Walter Mitty & Company's.

And when you're done, when you've reviewed all of the components of the Financial Report prepared just for him, you ask him this question: "Of the options we've suggested here, Mr. Jackson, which do you feel would best serve you right now?" And you wait for the answer, because the next person who speaks is going to make a purchase. If that's you, you're going to buy a "no sale".

And that's all, except for writing up the sale.

Of course there's everything else to do. What happens when the prospect says this? What happens when the prospect asks me that? And so forth. But believe me, whether you're selling sheets and pillow cases, computers, swimming pools, flowers and fertilizer, canaries, puppies, or quonset huts, the Power Selling Process will work.

How do I know that?

Because it already has!

But if the Process is to work for *you*, you must be willing to go through it the same way every single time. Using the same words the same way every time. Reviewing the Financial Report the same way every time.

And by doing it the same way every single time, you will not have a selling *person*, but a selling *system*. A Soft System. A completely predictable technology for producing formerly unpredictable results.

And you will be able to tell just how predictable it is through the use of an Information System.

Information Systems

For an Information System to interact with the above Soft System, it should provide you with the following information.

INFORMATION	BENCHMARK
How many calls were made?	*1*
How many prospects were reached?	*2*
How many appointments scheduled?	*3*
How many appointments confirmed?	*4*
How many appointments held?	*5*
How many Needs Analysis Presentations scheduled?	*6*
How many Needs Analyses confirmed?	*7*
How many Needs Analyses completed?	*8*
How many Solutions Presentations scheduled?	*9*
How many Solutions Presentations confirmed?	*10*
How many Solutions Presentations completed?	*11*

The information should be recorded on a form, either manually or as a data base on your computer.

The Information System will track the activity of your Selling System from Benchmark to Benchmark.

It will tell you an astonishing number of things.

It could tell you the rate of conversion between any two Benchmarks in your Selling Process. It could tell you at which Benchmark any particular salesperson needs help. Which of your people are "on the system"—that is, using the Selling System verbatim—and which ones are off it.

If you had calculated the cost of making a call, you could then calculate the cost of completing the next Benchmark in the process, and from that derive the next, and so on until you calculate the actual cost of making one sale.

In short, the Information System could tell you the things you need to know!

Things you don't know now.

Things you need to know in order to develop, control, and change your Selling System.

And things you also need to know in Finance and Production and Product Development.

If your Systems Strategy is the glue that holds your Franchise Prototype together, then information is the glue that holds your Systems Strategy together.

It tells you when and why you need to change.

Without it, you might as well put on a blindfold, have someone turn you around three times, and set out with a dart in your hand, waiting for a signal from the heavens to throw it.

Not a very promising game.

But one, it seems, most people in business are determined to play.

■ ■

Hard Systems, Soft Systems, Information Systems.

Things, actions, ideas, information.

The stuff of which our lives are made, and the stuff of your business as well.

Do you see how difficult it is to separate one from the other?

Do see how intertwined they are?

Do you now understand what I mean by your business system?

And why it is absolutely essential that you begin to think of your business as a fully integrated system?

That to approach any part of your business as though it were separate from all the rest would be lunacy, because everything in your business affects everything else in your business.

That your Primary Aim and your Strategic Objective and your Organizational Strategy and your Management Strategy and your People Strategy and your Marketing Strategy and your Systems Strategy—all of them are totally *interdependent*, rather than *independent* of one another?

That the success of your Business Development Program totally depends on your acceptance of that integration?

And that your Prototype *is* that integration?

If you understand all of that, then this book has been worth our time.

If you don't, take off the blindfold, because there's no going around one more time.

We've got business to attend to.

There's no time left to trust a dart in the dark.

"BRINGING THE DREAM BACK TO AMERICAN BUSINESS"

"You should know now that a man of knowledge lives by acting, not by thinking about acting, nor by thinking about what he will think when he has finished acting. A man of knowledge chooses a path with heart and follows it."

Carlos Castaneda
A Separate Reality

This book is not simply a prescription for success; *it's a call to arms.*

But this call to arms is not a call to do battle. It's a call to learning.

How to feel, think, and act differently and more productively, more *humanly* than our existing skills and understanding allow.

Today's world is a difficult place. Mankind has experienced more change in the past twenty years than in the 2,000 that preceded them.

Boundaries that once served us—geographically, politically, socially, emotionally—no longer exist. The rules are constantly changing. But people cannot live without boundaries, without structure, without rules. So new ones have sprung up and proliferated in order to fill the void left by the those that no longer seem to serve our "new age" condition.

156

Unfortunately, in a world of accelerated change there is little time for rules to take hold. As soon as the new rules are upon us, they too are swallowed up in the insatiable vortex of change, followed all too quickly by more rules, and then still more.

The result of all this change is chaos and disorder, each change bringing with it an even more turbulent world than the one before it with fewer and fewer traditions to hold on to. A world in trouble, where confusion reigns.

But the trouble didn't start "out there" in the world.

If it did, we'd *really* be in trouble. Because who among us knows enough to control or even have an impact on what's happening "out there?" If it is so difficult for us to do anything about our *businesses,* how in the world are we going to do anything about the *world?*

We can't. It's that simple. And any call to arms that suggests we can is a stop-gap measure, a call to disillusionment and ultimately to disaster. Because our stop-gap measures are not solutions. Our feeble attempts to fix the world can't change the overall condition. If they work at all, they can only change the circumstances in which we find ourselves at any given moment.

No, we can't change the world "out there." And fortunately, we don't have to; we can begin much closer to home. We can begin "in here." In fact, if we're to succeed, we must. Because the chaos isn't "out there" in everyone else. It's not "out there" in the world. The chaos is "in here" in you and me.

The *world's* not the problem, *you and I* are.

The *world's* not in chaos, *we* are.

The world's apparent chaos is only a reflection of our own inner turmoil.

If the world reflects a lack of good sense, it's because each one of us reflects the same. If the world acts as if it doesn't know what it's doing, it's because each one of us acts the same. If the world is violent, and greedy, and heartless, and inhuman, and often just plain stupid, it is because you and I are that way.

So if the world is going to be changed, we must first change our lives!

Unfortunately, we haven't been taught to think that way. We are an "out there" society, accustomed to thinking in terms of *them* against *us*. We want to fix the world so that we can remain the same. And for an "out there" society, coming "inside" is a problem.

But now is the time to learn how. Now is the time to change.

Because unless we do, the chaos will remain.

And we can't afford this kind of chaos much longer.

We're simply running out of time.

Bridging the Gap

And that's what this book is really about. Bridging the gap.

Between the "outside" and the "inside."

Between the world "out there" and the world "in here."

And your business can become that bridge. The bridge between you and the world. The bridge that can draw together the world "out there" and the world "in here" in such a way as to make both more human. In such a way that makes both more productive. In such a way that makes both worlds work.

For like the Boss's hotel, your business can become your *dojo*, your practice hall. Joe Hyams, in his book *Zen in the Martial Arts*, tells us what a *dojo* is:

A dojo is a miniature cosmos where we make contact with ourselves—our fears, anxieties, reactions, and habits. It is an arena of confined conflict where we confront an opponent who is not an opponent but rather a partner engaged in helping us understand ourselves more fully. It is a place where we can learn a great deal in a short time about who we are and how we react in the world. The conflicts that take place inside the dojo help us handle conflicts that take place outside. The total concentration and discipline required to study martial arts carries over to daily life. The activity in the dojo calls on us to constantly attempt new things, so it is also a source of learning—in Zen terminology, a source of self-enlightenment.[1]

And that is exactly what a small business is!

A small business is a place that responds instantly to any action we take. A place where we can practice implementing ideas in a way that changes lives. A place where we can begin to test all of the assumptions we have about ourselves. It is a place where questions are at least as important as answers, if not more so. It is a place where generalizations must give way to specifics. It is a place that demands our attention. A place where rules must be followed, and order preserved. A place that is practical, not idealistic. But a place where idealism must be present for the practical to serve. It is a place where the world is reduced to manageable size. Small enough to be responsive, but big enough to test everything we have. A true practice hall.

A world of our own.

---

1. Joe Hyams, *Zen in the Martial Arts* (Los Angeles: J. P. Tarcher, Inc., 1979), p. 12.

A World of Our Own

And that after all is the "Dream of American Business," the dream that has served as the catalyst for so many entrepreneurial (and not so entrepreneurial) efforts.

To create a world of our own.

What is this Entrepreneurial Revolution people are talking about today, where countless millions of us are going into business for ourselves?

It's nothing more than a flight from the world of chaos "out there" into a world of our own.

It's a yearning for structure, for form, for control. And for something else as well. Something more personal. Something less distinct, yet much more intimately connected with who we are as human beings. It's a yearning for relationship with ourselves and the world in a way impossible to experience in a job.

Unfortunately, as we've already seen, the "dream" is rarely realized; most businesses fail. And the reason is obvious. *We bring our chaos with us.*

We don't change. We try to change "out there." We try to change the world by starting a small business—*but we stay the same!*

And so the small business that was started to give us a new world becomes instead the worst job in the world!

The lesson to learn from all this is simple: We can't change our lives by starting "out there." All we can produce in the process is more chaos!

We can only change our lives and create a world of our own if we first understand how such a world is constructed, how it works, and the rules of the game. And that means we have to study the world and how we are in it. And in order to do that we need a world small enough in scope and complexity to study.

A small business is just such a world.

And a Business Development Program can be a means to study it most effectively.

And the Franchise Prototype can provide our study with the discipline it needs to succeed.

Innovation, Quantification, and Orchestration become the practice that brings us and our opponent—whoever that may be—to the discovery of our limits, our weaknesses, our strengths. To the discovery of what *really* works in the world rather than what our imaginations might wish would work. For in a martial arts contest, there is no room for imagination. We could get killed out there!

Innovation, Quantification, and Orchestration provide the belief system of our business, the philosophical bedrock of our interaction with the world. They become our source for learning, for creating, for expanding beyond our self-imposed limits.

And through Innovation, Quantification, and Orchestration our business can become something more than merely a place to go to work. It can become a place that satisfies more of ourselves than just The Technician. There is a place in Business Development for the whole of ourselves. For the innovator, for the maintainer, for the doer. For The Entrepreneur, The Manager, and The Technician in each one of us.

Our business *can* give us more life.

An Idea for Action

But does it work?

Will the model of the Franchise Prototype work for you?

There is an old Chinese proverb that says:

When you hear something, you will forget it.
When you see something, you will remember it.
But not until you do something, will you understand
it.

In short, my answer is a resounding, "Yes!" It does work. Every time it's applied. And it will work for you. It works because it requires the full engagement of the people working it. It can't be done half-heartedly. It can't be done frenetically. It can only be done intelligently, reasonably, intentionally, systematically, and compassionately.

The very *process* of Business Development creates instantaneous change in the people who engage in it.

And that is the key to its success.

Those who engage in the process must remember their aim in order to continue it. And in the process of remembering, their aim becomes tethered to something real in the world—their business. A place in which aims can be tested in a concrete, practical way. The business becomes a symbol for the life they wish to live, a visible manifestation of who they are and what they believe. A living, active, evolving testament to the will of man.

But, I ask you not to think about it any more.

It's time to act.

Because *until* you do, you won't understand it.

And *when* you do, there will be nothing left to think about—you'll be well on your way.

Until then, it's just another good idea, just another creative thought.

It's time to turn it into an innovation.

It's time to Bring the Dream Back to American Business.

It's been gone far too long.

About the Author

Michael E. Gerber is the CEO of The Michael Thomas Corporation, the multi-million-dollar company he founded in 1977 in San Mateo, California. The realization of a personal vision that has enhanced his and thousands of other businesspeople's lives, MTC has provided the The Michael Thomas Business Development Program to thousands of small companies, and is fast becoming the largest resource of its kind for small business in America.

Business visionary, entrepreneur, salesman, and manager, Michael E. Gerber has spoken throughout the country to business audiences about how to "Bring the Dream Back to American Business." His message is compelling and pragmatic. And best of all, as his thousands of clients attest, it works.

COMPLIMENTARY
SMALL BUSINESS NEEDS ANALYSIS
APPLICATION FORM

To secure a telephone appointment for a complimentary analysis of your small business, complete the following form by **PRINTING** the information requested, and return same along with a self-addressed stamped envelope to:

THE MICHAEL THOMAS CORPORATION
BUSINESS ANALYSIS DIVISION
1900 South Norfolk, Suite 301
San Mateo, California 94403

Or call:

THE MICHAEL THOMAS CORPORATION
BUSINESS ANALYSIS DIVISION
(415) 572-1335

YES, I HAVE READ *THE E-MYTH*, AND I WOULD LIKE TO PARTICIPATE IN A COMPLIMENTARY ANALYSIS OF MY SMALL BUSINESS.

MY NAME IS: _____

MY BUSINESS' NAME IS: _____

MY HOME ADDRESS IS: Street: _____

City: _____ State: _____ Zip: _____

MY BUSINESS ADDRESS IS: Street: _____

City: _____ State: _____ Zip: _____

MY HOME PHONE IS: ( ) _____ - _____

MY BUSINESS PHONE IS: ( ) _____ - _____

MY BUSINESS IS A: SOLE PROPRIETORSHIP ☐ CORPORATION ☐ PARTNERSHIP ☐ FAMILY BUSINESS ☐

MY BUSINESS DOES (Describe the kind of products, services your sell):

_____

_____

_____

I HAVE OWNED THIS BUSINESS FOR _____ YEARS

MY KEY BUSINESS FRUSTRATIONS ARE: NOT ENOUGH TIME ☐ NOT ENOUGH CUSTOMERS ☐ NOT ENOUGH PROFIT ☐ NOT ENOUGH PERSONAL INCOME ☐ CAN'T FIND GOOD PEOPLE ☐ CAN'T MANAGE THE PEOPLE I'VE GOT ☐ ALL OF THE ABOVE ☐